P-BOAT PILOT

Also by Robert Carlisle
Tower, This Is Andy and Other Flying Stories

P-Boat Pilot

With a Patrol Squadron in the Battle of the Atlantic

LIEUTENANT ROBERT L. CARLISLE
USNR (RET.)

FOREWORD BY
VICE ADMIRAL ALEXANDER S. HEYWARD, JR.
USN (RET.)

FITHIAN PRESS
SANTA BARBARA • 1993

Copyright ©1993 by Robert L. Carlisle
All rights reserved
Printed in the United States of America

Book design and typography by Jim Cook

Published by Fithian Press
Post Office Box 1525
Santa Barbara, California 93102

LIBRARY OF CONGRESS CATALOGING-IN-PUBLICATION DATA
Carlisle, Robert L.
   P-boat pilot: with a patrol squadron in the battle of the Atlantic /
Robert L. Carlisle
     p. cm.
   ISBN 1-56474-046-3
    1. Carlisle, Robert L., 1920– . 2. World War, 1939-1945—Aerial operations, American. 3. World War, 1939-1945—Naval operations, American. 4. World War, 1939-1945—Personal narratives, America 5. United States. Navy—Biography. 6. Air pilots, Military—United States—Biography. 7. World War, 1939-1945—Campaigns—Atlantic Ocean. I. Title.
D790.C274   1993
940.54'4973'092—dc20   92-33211
[B]   CIP

To my older brother, 1st Lieutenant Frank W. Carlisle, Jr., who, with his crew, was lost on January 9, 1945, when his B-25 was shot down during an attack on Japanese-held Clark Field, Philippine Islands.

Contents

Foreword	11
Preface	13

Part I: Peace
Ensign Curran	17
Student	19

Part II: Learning Time
Civilian Pilot Training	23
Fall, 1941	26
December 7, 1941	28

Part III: War
1942	33
UPF-7	35
"Yew'llbesorryeee!"	36
Lt. Boscetti	38
Swimming Sub-Squad	39
Russian Commandos	41
Thanksgiving 1942	43
NAS Norman	44
Solo	46

Part IV: Reaching The Goal
Night Flight	51
Flying Aces	52
Corpus	54
Decisions, Decisions	56
Squadron 18	58
Premonition	60
Lt. Lesgalier	61
FDR	63

Nav Flight	65
Wings of Gold	67
Bombsight	68
Branded	70
Norfolk, Virginia	72
Spirit of St. Vitis II	74
Deland	76
Rum-Runner	77
To Natal	79
Spike	81
Lonely Ascension Island	83
Short-Snorter	85
Patrol Squadron 73	86
Love	88
Agadir, French Morocco	90
Gibraltar	92
The Fiats	94
Aircraft Identification	96
Iowa	97
On Being a Co-Pilot	99
Sing-Along	101
P-Boat vs. Condor	104
Christmas 1943	106
Happy Hour	107
ROOWB	109
Torpedoes	111
Open Sea Landing	113

Part V: 1944

NAS Floyd Bennett	117
Blimp	119
Coast Guard	121
Bombs Away	122
Lend Lease	124
Leigh Light	126
Tassel Tess	128

Part VI: 1945

Mr. Hay	133
L.E. Smith	134
Collateral Duty	136
Iced Up	138
Garbage	140
Jeep Carrier	141
Bridges	143
U-235	145
Redeployed	147
VP-91	149
Potpourri	151
VE-VJ Day	153

Glossary   155

A section of photographs follows page 48

ODE TO THE PBY

Blessings on thee, PBY,
Staggering through the stormy sky,
Struts and fittings bent and worn,
With all fabric ripped and torn,
Rivets loose and flapping wings,
Leaky hull, 'mongst other things,
Your engines spit and pop like heck,
It's twelve more hours 'til they get checked.
When the airspeed meter climbs,
Past a rate of eighty-nine,
The crew's hearts sink into their boots,
As they don Mae Wests and parachutes.
Hull bottom ripped on jagged rocks,
Wing floats strewn upon the docks,
Paint all gone from landings hot,
Rivets popped from full-stall squats.
Control wires slack, and bulkheads bent,
Blisters cracked, their framework rent.
Oft I wonder, when on high,
How it is you still can fly,
For every time I fly with you,
On foggy night or in morning dew,
I pray you will return with me,
And not let us crash into the sea.

—Anonymous

FOREWORD

As a Naval Aviator for about thirty-six years and a P-boat pilot for some seven of those, this collection of memories, anecdotes, and good sea stories brought back many nostalgic and happy memories of my own.

Anyone who has even thought about wanting to fly will feel a kindred spirit as Robert Carlisle recounts his childhood dreams about becoming a pilot; his working and saving to pay for his first lessons; his ups and downs in the process, and that thrill of finally being alone in the air with no instructor to bother you!

This having been accomplished while in his teens, it was natural for him to choose to be a military pilot when he completed Civilian Pilot Training early in World War II. His accounts of experiences there and later in the Naval Air Training Command will bring back memories for any one of the thousands who went that route.

His wartime experiences mirrored those of many of us who operated over the sealanes of the North Atlantic. Far different from the broad Pacific, but vital to the movement of men and materials for the war effort in Europe and Africa. The P-boat pilots and their compatriot crews did their full share in this effort.

The mark of a good story is the inclusion of the Who, What, When and Where involved in it. Robert Carlisle does this to a remarkable degree. Either he has a remarkable memory or he keeps a detailed diary—or both. He is a fine storyteller.

—VICE ADMIRAL ALEXANDER S. HEYWARD, JR.
USN (RET.)

PREFACE

I have been considering writing this story for many years, and now over fifty years have passed and I am just getting the story told. Many of today's citizens do not realize how close America and its allies were to defeat after the Japanese attack on Pearl Harbor. During the early months of 1942, German submarines, the "U-boats," inflicted grievous damage to shipping off the east coast of the United States. Virtually unopposed, the enemy underwater marauders sank hundreds of thousands of tons of vessels from New York to the coast of Florida. Some U-boats even penetrated into the Gulf of Mexico to the delta of the Mississippi.

At the height of the sinkings, Winston Churchill expressed the fear that his beleaguered island might fall because of the loss of food and war materials.

But the convoy system, the grouping of ships to sail together, escorted by war ships and airplanes, brought a halt to the U-boat menace.

This is the story of one squadron that helped win the Battle of the Atlantic—Navy Patrol Squadron 73.

VP-73 had been in action against the German U-boat even before Pearl Harbor. U.S. deployment to North Africa placed it in an area known to be a "happy hunting ground" for the enemy submarines, yet not one vessel escorted by Patrol Squadron 73 was ever attacked or sunk by enemy submarines.

—LIEUTENANT ROBERT L. CARLISLE, USNR (RET.)

Part I: Peace

10 April 1940—President Roosevelt extends maritime danger zone for U.S. ships, following the German invasion of Denmark and Norway the previous day.

1 July 1941—Squadron designation of Patrol Squadron 15 (VP-15) changed to Patrol Squadron 73 (VP-73). Lt. Cdr. James Edward Leeper USN named squadron Commander.

6 August 1941—Patrol Squadron 73 initiates routine air patrols from Reykjavik, Iceland, over North Atlantic convoy routes.

ENSIGN CURRAN

As he stood in our living room, Ensign Jack Curran looked as though he had stepped from a Norman Rockwell poster. Resplendent in his dress blues, untarnished gold braid and buttons, and Navy Wings on his chest, Jack appeared to be the epitome of an "All American Boy."
To me, he was that very thing.
A couple of years older than I, Jack had graduated from Sacred Heart High School in 1936. After attending Creighton University in Omaha, he enlisted in the Naval Aviation Cadet program, and after a year of rigorous training had just been commissioned an Ensign at the Navy flight school in Pensacola, Florida. At the same time he received his pilot's wings. This was his first leave since his graduation.
Prior to departing for pre-flight school, Jack wanted to show me how to fence. At Creighton he had taken up the sport. Since he had an épée and fencing mask, I ordered a fencing foil from Bill's Camera and Sporting Goods for $3.95. I made the fencing mask from stiff clothesline wire and fine wire mesh.
The day my rapier arrived, Jack received his orders to report to pre-flight school, and all hopes of dueling were put on hold.
Ensign Curran had an eager listener as he told of his experiences in flight training, his first solo, formation flying, instrument check-rides, dive-bombing practice, fighter tactics and all of the other wonderful things he had done and seen.
In those days, before Pearl Harbor, Navy pilots were given an opportunity to fly every type of operational plane used by the Fleet. Jack had flown them all.
Especially thrilling to me was his account of formation flying in an OS2U, a Vought Kingfisher.

He told of flying in formation so close to his wingman that he could touch the wing-tip float of his flying mate by gently rocking his wings.

As the afternoon wore on, Ensign Curran told countless stories of his experience as an Aviation Cadet. Then and there I made up my mind that I would become a Naval Aviator, just like Jack.

Finally, Jack's visit came to an end. As he climbed into his car, I turned to my dad and said, "I've got to get two years of college so I can be a Navy pilot like Jack." Dad agreed.

Reporting to flight duty at Corpus Christi Naval Air Station in Texas, Jack served as an instructor in VO/VS (battleship and cruiser scout planes, such as the OS2U Kingfisher). Following Pearl Harbor, Jack became a pilot for VIPs. After many flying assignments, Lt. Curran was the officer-in-charge of flight tests for a guided missile being perfected in 1944 at Floyd Bennett Field in New York. Code-named "Project Pelican," it entailed a wing-and-tail-equipped 500-pound bomb dropped from a Vega Ventura PV-1. A German-designed spinning reel paid out a wire attached to the missile. Electrical impulses fed via the wire to servo motors, which moved the control surfaces on the wing and tail surfaces, allowed the gliding bomb to be directed to the target. The missile was equipped with a magnesium flare fixed to the center of the wing to assist the operator in seeing it as it glided toward the objective.

As the war neared its end, Jack, now a Commander, was still denied an opportunity to serve with an operational squadron overseas. At long last, shortly before the signing of the peace aboard the *Missouri,* Jack was given command of a PV squadron stationed at Clark Field, in the Philippines. His squadron's mission was to locate isolated American or Japanese forces in the islands.

On one of these missions, Jack's PV slammed into a mountain during a driving tropical storm, and he and all of his crew perished.

Because of Jack Curran, I eventually became a P-boat pilot.

STUDENT

Classes at Wayne State Teachers College had been going for three weeks when I enrolled as a freshman. My older brother, Frank, had made arrangements. Since he was leaving Larson's Department Store in Wayne to manage the Fair Store in Norfolk, Larson's was in need of some extra help. For thirty dollars a month I would sell shoes in the ladies' shoe department, trim windows and do general janitorial work. I would work afternoons and on Saturdays and holidays, and go to college in the mornings. Mr. Larson took care of all of my college expenses, books, registrations and incidental fees. I was finally getting a chance to get the two years of schooling I needed to qualify for Navy flight training. It was September 1940.

As I enrolled for classes, I assumed that a Naval Aviator should have some college physics. I blithely enrolled in Physics I. Mind you, it had been over two years since I had taken a physics course at Norfolk Senior High, and my grades in high school physics were nothing to be proud of.

For three days I foundered in the Physics I class. I had no idea what the professor was talking about! I had trouble even locating the pages being referred to. Something had to be done, at once.

On the third day, rather than face another session of frustration, I went to the instructor's office and explained my plight. He was very understanding and sympathetic to my cause. He had a suggestion. He told me he had two students who roomed together at Terrace Hall, where I lived. They were both seniors, and were his best physics and science students. He suggested that I talk to them and see if they would tutor me in physics. At least now I had a ray of hope.

That evening after work I asked Mrs. Theobald, the house mother, for the room number of S—— and O——, the prospective tutors.

As I rapped on the door, I heard muffled laughing and the sound of chairs being shoved across the floor.

The door opened a crack, and I asked if S—— or O—— was there. The door opened, and I was told to step in.

Entering their quarters, I was flabbergasted . . . their room was draped in heavy tapestries, looking for all the world like a sultan's harem tent! A hookah sat on the floor amid a ring of velvet pillows. Candles were everywhere.

The two were holding photographs in each hand, and laughing over something. I thought for a moment they were laughing at me. Then I saw what was so humorous. It was the photographs they held!

They were taking pictures of each other, front view, *au naturel.* The two explained that they had rigged up a darkroom in their closet, complete with all the necessary developing equipment. They had processed the photos themselves, and the two of them seemed immensely pleased with the results. Especially in making comparisons, one with the other.

All thoughts of these two tutoring me vanished at once.

By eight o'clock the next morning I was standing in the professor's office. In short order, I explained that I would be unable to take advantage of the tutors, and that I planned on dropping Physics I and taking a course in something I had a chance of passing. He had no objections.

The trip to the registrar was productive. My schedule included Introduction to Education, Speech, English Literature, Mechanical Drawing, and Meteorology. At least that class in the study of the weather ought to help a potential Naval Aviator.

And I would have absolutely no need for any tutors.

Part II: Learning Time

27 May 1941—President Roosevelt declares a state of unlimited national emergency; he also extends range of Neutrality Patrol.

16 August 1941—Lt. Gerald Duffy of VP-73 sights the first German submarine. This is properly reported. The British later capture it.

27 November 1941—"War warning" message by CNO Admiral Harold R. Stark, sent to Commanders of Pacific and Atlantic Fleets.

7 December 1941—Japanese attack Pearl Harbor. President Roosevelt orders mobilization.

8 December 1941—The United States declares war on Japan. Gunboat *Wake* becomes first and only U.S. warship in the second World War to surrender.

CIVILIAN PILOT TRAINING

I avidly read the last issue of the WSTC newspaper, the *Goldenrod*. A feature story told of the college inaugurating a summer Civilian Pilot Training Program. It was late spring, 1941.

According to the story, the CPT would give both flight training and ground instruction amounting to $365 to be paid by the federal government. The only expense to the trainee would be $6 for the physical examination and $7.20 for an accident insurance policy. Ten students would be accepted.

I immediately went to the registrar's office in the ad building, where Miss Smothers supplied me with the necessary forms.

By carefully budgeting my funds, I was able to pay Dr. Walter Benthack the price of the flight physical. Further budgeting enabled me to finance the insurance.

All of the flying was done at the Wayne Municipal Airport under the tutelage of Mr. Stanley Fuller, who operated the flying school at the airfield. Fuller lived in Storm Lake, Iowa, and each Monday morning he flew to the Wayne airport in his Lockheed Vega, left it tied down beside the hangar until Friday, then flew back to Storm Lake for the weekend. Not a single one of us ever went over and examined the Vega during its stay. Today's pilots would never ignore a plane like the Lockheed.

The ground school was conducted by Mr. Arthur Gulliver, principal of the training school. Taught in the science building, the ground school was memorable. We ten struggled to learn about power plants, instruments, theory of flight, meteorology, navigation, Morse code and all of the other things a pilot was required to know.

Ground school was complicated by a curious speech habit of Mr. Gulliver. He would end nearly every sentence with "Howmanysee?" He always said it as though the three words were one. One evening I counted 361 "Howmanysees" asked in one lecture period.

During the summer term the coeds could stay out until 9:30 P.M. At that time they had to be safely ensconced within the walls of Pile or Neihardt Halls.

At nine o'clock, ground school over, we ten would casually emerge from the classroom, walk down the steps of the science building out into the presence of a dozen or so coeds breathlessly awaiting our emergence. Some of us wore shirts, ties, trousers and shoes of a semi-military cut, and we talked amongst ourselves (but loud enough for the girls to hear) about "angle of attack," "drift angle," "power-on and power-off stalls," "Venturi" and all sorts of aviation terms designed to impress the coeds.

There was no doubt about it, we oozed Glamour with a capital "G."

We were the pilots.

Out at the airport we weren't so glamorous. There were no coeds to impress, and our flight instructors were beyond the impressionable stage.

Upon reporting to the Wayne Municipal Airport for the first day of Civilian Pilot Training, we discovered that we would receive our lessons in Aeronca Chief airplanes. They were in the same category as the Piper Cubs that Andy Risser used in his flying school. I didn't think I would have any trouble switching over to the Aeroncas after soloing and flying the Cubs at Risser's. I didn't.

Though out at the flying field we didn't have Mr. Gulliver and his "howmanysees" to confuse and distract us, those of us who had Slim Halgrimson as our flight instructor experienced a bit of difficulty.

Slim was a rancher from western Nebraska. He flew in to Wayne in a Piper Cub with the word "Slim" painted on the underside of the right wing and the upper surface of the left wing. When out coyote hunting, he said, he wanted the ranchers to know who was flying around.

Slim was all of six feet three, with a thin, gangly build. In the training planes, the student occupied the rear seat, the instructor sat in the front. When Slim was properly seated in the plane, the hapless student pilot in the rear could not view the instrument panel, as Slim's bony knees projected up so the student could see little of the plane's dashboard. The matter was further complicated by the western hat he insisted upon wearing. No matter how Slim scrunched down, the student could see nothing ahead. Slim attempted to alleviate the condition by loosening his seat belt and sitting on the edge of his seat, pressed against the side of the cockpit. It helped a little, but not much.

In spite of these problems, the CPT course proceeded without a hitch.

I particularly enjoyed the portion of the flight syllabus dealing with spins. Perhaps this was because during the spin lessons we were obliged to wear parachutes. Wearing the chutes gave us a feeling of security, though I doubt if we could have got out of the plane to use them.

On one of my solo flights I was scheduled to practice spins and spin recovery. Once aloft and in the practice area north of Wayne, I made the two clearing turns, pulled the carburetor heat, retarded the throttle and eased back on the stick. As the airspeed dropped, I held the nose high, and when the buffeting hit the plane, I gave full right rudder. The Aeronca slewed to the right and the nose-down gyrations began.

I counted, "1, 1/2, 2, 1/2, 3, 1/2, 4." At "four," I neutralized the rudder, popped the stick forward, and the ship came out of the spin, in a dive. The speed rapidly built up. As the airspeed needle neared the red line, I gingerly pulled back on the stick and came out of the dive. The g-forces pushed me against the seat, and I looked out at the wing tips. It seemed as though they were bending upward at least a foot from the strain of the pull-out. I'd let too much speed build up during the recovery.

That spin recovery scared me. I thought I might have to use that chute. An ashen-faced CPT Cadet landed, and saying nothing, left for his room at Terrace Hall.

As summer school neared its end, the CPT program also neared its finish. During August we were scheduled to take our final check rides with the Civil Aeronautics Administration (now the FAA) examiners. They arrived on August 21 in a bit of a snit. It seemed they were behind schedule, and would not have time to ride with all ten of us for the flight test. They decided to fly three students, and if they passed, they would assume we all were of their ability, and we would all pass. They selected Nygren, McKay and Mitchell. They passed the flight test with flying colors. So did the rest of us.

FALL, 1941

With the Civilian Pilot Training Program over, my flying days came to an abrupt halt. Renting a plane was expensive for a college student earning thirty dollars a month selling ladies' shoes. To rent a plane cost six dollars an hour!

The war situation didn't look good. On September 1 the Navy had assumed responsibility for trans-Atlantic convoys from Argentia to the meridian of Iceland; on September 11 the Navy issued an order to "shoot on sight"; on September 26 the Navy ordered protection of all merchant shipping in U.S. defensive waters.

Despite the ominous war news, Wayne State College held its annual homecoming in October. Jack Loisel called me and said he was coming over to Wayne, and for me to meet him at the College Inn just off campus. He had a date with Frances Meyers, an old friend of mine.

Jack had just been commissioned and had received his wings in the Army Air Corps. As we sat and talked over Cokes, Lt. Loisel told me that he was heading for the Philippines, where he was assigned to a heavy bombardment squadron flying the latest bomber used by the Air Corps, the B-17 "Flying Fortress."

Almost completely ignoring our dates, Jack and I discussed my chances of being accepted into Aviation Cadet training by either the Army or the Navy.

Jack tried to convince me that the military services were only

LEARNING TIME

looking for "good, average" pilots, and that the "Superman" thinking was out.

But despite Jack's encouraging words, I still doubted that I would ever qualify either mentally or physically for flight training.

Then an item in the newspaper told of a committee organized by a Clayton Knight that was being formed to recruit American air crews and pilots for the Royal Air Force and Royal Canadian Air Force. According to the article, qualifications for flight training in those services were not as stringent as ours.

In response to the news item, I wrote the Canadian Ministry in Washington for information concerning enlistment in the RAF.

According to the Ministry, the Clayton Knight Committee was their main recruiting agency, and now an American would not lose his citizenship by joining a foreign army, since the RAF required allegiance to itself, and not to the British government.

I wanted to fly, and I didn't care whose insignia adorned the wings of my plane, provided it was Allied.

On November 13 my date and I went to the movie *Yank in the RAF*. It inspired me more than ever to try to enter the Royal Air Force. It's a cinch I wasn't going to be drafted into the walking army.

On November 26, 1941, a large Japanese task force secretly departed from an unfrequented bay in the Kuriles. The fleet included six large, fast carriers, two new battleships, two heavy cruisers and a screen of a light cruiser and nine destroyers. Three submarines had gone ahead, and eight tankers and supply ships accompanied the armada in order to replenish it.

The fleet's destination was unknown.

On November 27, Admiral Harold R. Stark, Chief of Naval Operations, sent a "War Warning" message to the Commanders of the Pacific and Asiatic fleets.

On December 6, convoys carrying the Japanese Army for the invasion of Malaya were sighted by an American PBY from the Philippines, and later by an Australian Hudson reconnaissance aircraft from Malaya.

The Japanese landings in Malaya and Siam therefore came as no surprise. The "Day of Infamy" was near.

DECEMBER 7, 1941

The 1941 Christmas buying season started early. As the first weekend of December neared, Larson's Department Store was doing a land-office business. Especially in the ladies' shoe department where I worked. It was after eleven o'clock when we put the last shoe box on the shelf and I headed for my room at the Johnsons'.

I wanted to get home and get some sleep, as semester tests were coming up and I planned on sacking out and studying all Sunday afternoon, to prove to my older brother, Frank, I was some sort of a student.

I was roused from a deep sleep by Mrs. Johnson calling me to the phone. It was from my brother Orv in Norfolk.

I sleepily answered the phone and asked, "What's going on?"

"The Japs bombed Pearl Harbor. We're at war with Japan," he almost yelled.

"Pearl Harbor, where the heck is Pearl Harbor?" I inquired.

"Somewhere in the Pacific Ocean, in Hawaii, I think," he replied. "Turn on your radio and listen to the news. I'm going to hang up now and hear what's going on." With that, he slammed his phone down and the call was over.

As Orv advised, I turned on my radio to hear more details of the Japanese air raid on the American naval base at Pearl Harbor. All thought of studying for the coming exams vanished with the news. My attitude was typical of most of the other male students at WSTC. We knew we couldn't finish school with a war on.

That night I wrote in my diary:

"Well, it happened. Japanese planes bombed Manila and the Hawaiin (sic) Islands. Japan declared war on the USA. I'm going to finish out the semester and join up. Heaven help me and every poor guy that is in the same boat. We must win. Those g—d—n Nazis and slant-eyed yellow b—ds are going to get it. God help us!"

On Monday, all of us skipped classes to hear President Roosevelt address the Senate and House and heard him ask for a declaration of war against Japan.

Some of the fellows wanted to march down to the recruiting offices then and there and join up—a task that would have required quite a bit of a march, since the nearest recruiter for any of the services was located in Norfolk, some thirty-five miles away.

Still convinced in my own mind that I lacked the mental and physical requirements for flight training in either the Army Air Corps or the Navy, I sent off to Lincoln for a copy of my birth certificate so I would have some of the paperwork necessary to enlist in the Royal Air Force. Bev Canning and Bob Eckert planned on going with me to Canada in January—provided we could arrange bus fare to the RCAF selection board in Winnipeg.

December was rapidly bringing 1941 to a close. On the twenty-third I wrote in my diary:

"I have done everything I wanted to do. Came to college, learned to fly . . . now with the U.S. at war, my future and that of all the fellows my age is sealed. If I do go, and if I don't get a chance to come back to either college or home, I have no regrets. I have been gathering the necessary papers for the RAF. It seems funny to think of going to war. Yet if we young fellows don't throw ourselves into this mess regardless of personal danger and sacrifice, the world won't be fit for any decent person to be in."

In 1942 I would have enough college hours to qualify for flight training. Then I would see if my fears concerning my fitness to be either a Navy or Air Corps pilot had any foundation.

Part III: War

22 June 1942—Plane 73-P-8, while covering convoy UR-29 is damaged by four direct hits from a U-boat's deck guns. Six of the nine crew members are wounded. The plane makes a forced water landing one mile from shore and beaches about sixty miles east of Kaldadarnes, Iceland. Villagers aid in the rescue of the crew.

8 November 1942—Allies invade North Africa.

10 November 1942—U.S. warships and carrier aircraft engage French naval forces at Casablanca, Morocco. Oran, Algeria surrenders to the U.S. forces. Allied-French armistice signed.

13 November 1942—Navy Patrol Squadron 73 begins operations from French Morocco.

1942

The war was certainly going badly for the United States and its allies in the South Pacific. The Japanese forces seemed invincible.

My brother Orville left for the Army at 11:00 A.M. on January 13. He was to report to Fort Crook in Omaha. Clayton Andrews was in the same contingent. Orv was rejected because of a heart murmur and a bad back. He would have a tough job staying at home while all of his friends were out fighting the war.

My older brother, Frank, had been reclassified to 1B; then, for some unknown reason, he was put in the 1A category.

My draft number put me in the upper sixth, but I wouldn't wait to be drafted into the walking army. I wanted to fly!

I finally got all of the necessary papers together to send the Knight Committee in Kansas City. Bev Canning, Bob Eckert and I planned on going there next week to take the physicals and fill out the final papers, provided we could get enough money to pay the bus fare, $21.73.

Frank was notified he would go April 23, 1942; I still heard nothing of my status.

I made an inquiry about applying for flight training in the Navy, but was turned down because I didn't have enough college hours. It took sixty to even qualify for entrance.

By May 1, I had the necessary college hours and, with great apprehension, I went to Chief Cash of the Norfolk Navy Recruiting Station to enlist in the Navy as an Aviation Cadet.

I passed all of the preliminary tests and became a Seaman Second Class, V-5, USNR. My next stop would be the Aviation Cadet Selection Board in Kansas City, where I reported on May 20, 1942.

For a small-town boy, being in a metropolis like Kansas City was quite a thrill. Even more of a thrill was the rocket-like ride in the elevator up to the Selection Board offices.

A battery of Navy corpsmen punched, poked, pinched and peeked into every portion of my anatomy. Another detachment confronted me with a battery of written and oral tests to determine my mental acuity. I passed all of the evaluations with flying colors and, when I was fully clothed again, I was summoned before the officer-in-charge for the swearing-in ceremony.

As I raised my right hand, one of the corpsmen came breathlessly into the room and, interrupting the proceedings, informed the Lieutenant that I was sixteen pounds underweight and couldn't be enlisted. I was crestfallen.

The corpsmen said if I drank a lot of buttermilk, cokes or water, I might be able to gain the weight. "Or," he said, "eat a bunch of bananas." Bananas made more sense to me.

Rapid calculations convinced me I needed more than sixteen pounds of bananas to do the job, because half their weight was in the peels. Twenty-six pounds ought to do the trick, I thought. Luckily I found a grocery store in the middle of downtown Kansas City, made my purchase of twenty-six pounds of bananas and immediately began eating them.

I ate the last one as I punched the "up" button on the elevator. The corpsman, seeing the determined look on my face, lost no time in reweighing me. He smiled as he turned to me and said, "You're in."

After the induction ceremonies, the Lieutenant handed me my orders, stating that I would begin my preliminary training in Secondary Civilian Pilot Training at Morningside College in Sioux City on July 15, 1942. I was an Aviation Cadet at last!

I ate my next banana in December of 1988. My doctor said they contain a lot of potassium, which I needed. I must have been awfully healthy in 1942.

UPF-7

Rickenbacker Field in Stevens, South Dakota, had been established in the early 'twenties, and was now being operated by Graham Flying Service. E.L. Graham, a contemporary of Andy Risser, owned the aviation school and was assisted by his sons, Junior, who was the chief flight instructor, Hewitt, who was in charge of the maintenance and Ralph, who was in charge of the flight line. Several other flight instructors were also retained. Morningside College furnished the ground school instruction.

Both Primary Civilian Pilot Training, like the one I had completed in Wayne, and Secondary CPT were taught at Graham's. The students were Army and Navy Cadets. Both ground school and flight instruction began on July 15, 1942. The Primary CPT flights were made in J-3 Cubs, and the Secondary CPT, in which I was enrolled, flew Waco UPF-7s. With its two wings and huge radial engine, the UPF-7 certainly impressed all of us. With its wide-spread landing gear and blue and yellow paint job, it looked powerful and strong. It was.

Across the highway from the airport was a defunct nightclub, the Chez Paree. It was there that we ate, slept and studied.

We were issued khaki uniforms and overseas caps, and although we looked sort of military, when the instructors attempted to teach us how to march we looked like a rag-tag, motley mob. No one knew his right foot from his left, much to the despair of the D.I.

Our first introductory flights were made in a Waco 9, a much earlier and somewhat smaller version of the UPF-7. Once we mastered the 9, we were assigned the bigger UPF-7.

On August 6, 1942, I soloed the Waco UPF-7. From then on it was one aerobatic flight after another until I mastered spins, loops, rolls, Immelmanns, snap rolls, inverted flights and lazy-eights.

Of all of the cadets, I remember one above all, a fellow named Brooks. Brooks was from Norfolk, having moved there after I had gone to college. His father was the manager of a company in Norfolk. Brooks liked wings—the kind you pin on your shirt signifying you were a pilot.

On our first afternoon off, after we had soloed the UPF-7, we all went into Sioux City to see the sights. Brooks headed for the Army Surplus Store and purchased some wings to pin on his shirt. When he caught up with us he had wings on his left shirt pocket, wings and propeller insignia on both of his collar tabs, on both sides of his overseas cap and on both shirt cuffs. He had enough wings and propellers on that he didn't need a Waco to go flying!

On September 5, Secondary CPT was finished. I had 44.20 hours in the UPF-7 and felt like a real pilot.

Upon arriving home, I found a letter from the Navy, ordering me to report to the pre-flight school at St. Mary's College, Moraga, California, on September 17. At last I was going to the real Navy to become a Naval Aviator.

One afternoon before I left, I was in downtown Norfolk, and I met Brooks standing on the street corner. He was still wearing his khaki uniform and overseas cap, and no less than ten sets of wings and propellers!

On September 13, I boarded the train in South Norfolk bound for Kansas City and California. I hoped to return as an Ensign in the Naval Reserve, with a set of gold wings on my chest.

"YEW'LLBESORRYEEE!"

Railroad travel in 1942 was a triumph of ignorance over civilization. Coaches and Pullmans dating back to the Civil War were brought out of storage and used for troop transportation. Of this I am certain.

The coach we Cadets occupied on the trip to St. Mary's Pre-Flight School was one of those antiques. There were no electric lights, and gas or coal oil mantles hung from the ceiling and the walls. With great effort we pried open the windows in order to get some ventilation, and were rewarded with a shower of sand-like cinders cascading through the opening. The pillows, thoughtfully supplied by the Atchinson, Topeka and Santa Fe, soon turned a dirty gray. Our once-white tee-shirts soon took on the same hue, as did our faces and skin. There wasn't enough water either to drink or to wash with, and sanitary facilities would have done the "40 et 8's" of World War I proud.

On September 17 our train pulled into Moraga, California, the home of St. Mary's College, our pre-flight school. Thirty-seven gritty youths staggered from the train and were greeted by a detachment of sailors, each shouting orders to us as though we were about to enter a major naval engagement.

It was then that I discovered that a Naval Aviation Cadet was the lowest form of being in the entire world. Being neither officers nor enlisted men, we were in limbo. Everybody was senior and superior to us, even the newest Seamen Second Class could order us around—and they did.

Boarding the gray Navy buses, I noticed that some of the Cadets carried golf clubs and tennis rackets. They must have thought we were headed for a country club. They certainly got fooled.

As we disembarked in front of a wooden barracks, we were met by an officer who introduced himself as Lt. Frankie Albers. Thirty-six of the Cadets almost swooned over that information. Albers was a legendary football hero from Stanford. I had never heard of him, and I couldn't have cared less.

Still carrying our bags and meager belongings, we were marched to a small athletic field complete with chinning bars and a track. Here we were obliged to do push-ups, run an agility course, and do knee-bends. As a final test, we came to the chinning bars. Here Lt. Albers explained how to chin properly, then he leaped into the air, grabbed the bar, and proceeded to chin himself time and again. Occasionally he would do the chinning one-handed, talking all the time. He must have done it a hundred and fifty times! When it came our turn, we weren't as peppy. I think my record was four times.

As we were marched back to what were to be our barracks, we met a large formation of Cadets emerging from one of the nearby buildings. Hoots and catcalls greeted us. "Yew'llbesorryeee!" they shouted over and over. Despite this welcome from the upperclassmen, we were glad to finally be assigned bunks in Essex Hall. My address was imposing. It read: 8th Battalion, Company "C," 1st Platoon, Bunk 31.

The purpose of pre-flight was to develop physical condition through a program of athletics. I had never been one to engage in physical activities, and I had been too small and light to participate in either high school or college athletic events. Even the second team would have smashed me. As a result, I chose as my extracurricular activities speech, debate and oratory. About the only exercise I got was when I delivered a particularly stirring oration complete with gestures, raising of the voice and a bit of pacing.

Nonetheless, I was in the Navy now, an Aviation Cadet, and here I planned to stay. I was not about to quit.

LT. BOSCETTI

By my observation, the Navy had enlisted every athlete of any note, given them a basic indoctrination course, commissioned them and sent them to the pre-flight schools. Our battalion officer was one of those athletes. Though I hadn't seen too many real athletes in my time, Lt. Boscetti possessed genuine physical prowess.

Lt. Boscetti's conduct on the five-mile cross-country run demonstrated his stamina. The entire battalion would be jogging down the roadway. Lt. Boscetti not only set the pace for the run, but he matched the speed of the pack, step by step. Occasionally he would jog to the head of the column, shout some words of encouragement, then run to the back of the mob, exhorting the laggards to speed it up, then to the middle of the column, talking, encouraging and commenting as he ran. I do believe he covered ten times the distance we did by running back and forth that way. And he never took a deep breath!

It was also impossible to fool him. I found that out the hard way.

One of the courses we were subjected to was boxing. Cadet Kenneth Carlon and I were paired and scheduled to put on a match of three two-minute rounds. Ken occupied the bunk below me, and we were good friends. Anticipating the coming boxing exhibition, we talked over the problem. Neither of us wanted to get hurt—a black eye, or a bloody nose or whatever damage might be inflicted on us. Being bunk-mates, we sought a way out of the problem. We decided that we would dance around, throw punches at the empty air, grimace fiercely and act like we were really mixing it up, but without landing a single punch. We shook on it, making it a gentleman's agreement.

On the day of the bout, Ken and I climbed into the ring. Lt. Boscetti was the referee. After giving us instructions, he retired to a corner, the bell rang and the battle was on!

For about a minute and a half of the first round, we two jigged, danced, leaped, snorted, wheezed and swung at each other, careful not to land a solitary punch. Soon our arms were so tired we could barely lift the heavy mitts. But still there was no contact.

As we stood there, our arms hanging limply at our sides, weighed down by the heavy gloves, Lt. Boscetti shouted to us to "get in there and mix it up!!" I turned to look at him, when—*pow*—Carlon landed one right on my kisser. I went down like a poled ox, feeling and seeing nothing. A few minutes later, thoroughly doused with water, I revived to face a hysterical Lt. Boscetti. He was laughing so hard he almost fell over the ring ropes and onto the floor.

Aviation Cadet Kenneth Carlon proved to me that he was no gentleman, and I never let him forget what he had done to me. I was the most indignant bunk-mate in the Navy.

Lt. Boscetti never mentioned our attempt to fool him. He didn't have to; both Ken and I knew what we had been up to.

SWIMMING SUB-SQUAD

Inasmuch as the Navy spent most of its time around water, it required that all of the Aviation Cadets meet certain minimum requirements in the area of swimming. A Cadet could be discharged for failing to learn how to swim, as well as for any other reason. Therefore, shortly after reporting to St. Mary's, all of the Cadets were subjected to a battery of tests to determine their agility, strength and general athletic prowess. Foremost among these tests was swimming.

I failed the swimming test. In fact, I almost drowned. There was no way I could bluff my way out of it the way Carlon and I had tried to do in boxing. I was assigned to the Swimming Sub-Squad. I was not alone. A bus load of non-swimmers were lined up outside of Essex Hall. It was a cold, misty morning, and even in our uniforms, we were so cold our teeth chattered. And we were going for a swim—where, we didn't know.

When everyone was aboard, Lt. Boscetti vaulted into the bus and announced that, since the swimming pool at the college was in use, we were going to a private estate for our natation. He went on to explain that a wealthy couple in Moraga, feeling the need to do something to help the war effort, had donated the use of their Olympic-sized swimming pool to St. Mary's Pre-Flight School.

Our bus was admitted through the wrought iron gate by a liveried guard, and soon stopped at the pool. To us, it looked like a mosaic-lined ocean!

As the mist swirled about us, and the wind moaned in the trees, we shed our uniforms and put on our swim trunks. Any idea that some of us might have had of the luxury of a swim in California vanished post-haste. We about froze. One of my fellow sufferers in the Swimming Sub-Squad was Cadet Harold Buddenbohm, from Effingham, Kansas.

In the swimming department, Bood really had a problem. He had no natural buoyancy! Whereas a normal body in the water has some tendency to float, Bood had none. When he jumped into the pool he went directly to the bottom, and could walk around on the floor of the pool for as long as he could hold his breath. In order to pass the "Five Minute Float," Bood had to really thrash and tread with both his hands and legs to stay on the surface. At the end of the float test, he was worn out.

With a great deal of perseverance we all successfully graduated from the sub-squad. We mastered the breast stroke, the crawl, the back-stroke, underwater and all of the other strokes deemed by the Navy to be vital in order to survive. We were taught how to use cargo nets to abandon ship, and how to jump from a sinking vessel, using a twelve-foot tower as a substitute ship. As each Cadet stood at the edge of the tower platform, Lt. Boscetti would yell, "Grab your family jewels and jump!" Without exception each Cadet covered that portion of his anatomy and leaped feet first into the pool.

Except one. He grabbed his nose.

RUSSIAN COMMANDOS

Lt. Boscetti was apologetic as he addressed our battalion mustered for morning quarters in front of our barracks.

Tomorrow, Saturday, at 1300 (1 P.M., in Navy talk) we would all go on our first liberty. We had been restricted to the confines of the school since we arrived four weeks ago. This would be our first opportunity to go "ashore."

Everything was in order, with one exception. Lt. Boscetti explained that our dress blue uniforms, required for shore leave, had not yet arrived from the tailor and would not be available for our Saturday liberty.

One hundred and fifty disappointed Aviation Cadets groaned as one. The lack of dress blues threatened to keep us all confined to the base. Whoever said "war is hell" sure knew what he was talking about.

"But," Lt. Boscetti continued, "liberty will still be granted to all Cadets of the 8th Battalion wearing the Class Blue Baker uniform of the day."

The Blue Baker uniform was nondescript. It consisted of a khaki shirt, black tie, green marine trousers, heavy suede "boondocker" combat boots and a Marine overseas cap. In the cool weather of San Francisco, a dark blue pull-over jacket was worn, devoid of any insignias of rank or branch of service.

Although we had all hoped to appear on the streets of San Francisco in our dress blues so that the Californians could see what real Aviation Cadets looked like, we betrayed no disappointment on having to wear the Blue Baker uniform. The main consideration was, we would get liberty!

On Saturday the battalion piled into a fleet of Navy buses and set off for San Francisco. As we rode into the city, one of the Cadets became our song leader and a chorus of boisterous Navy songs filled the air. "Bell Bottomed Trousers," "O'Reilly's Daughter," "You'll Never Get to Heaven" and dozens of other songs rang through the bus.

Finally arriving at the USO canteen, we clambered off the buses and the one hundred and fifty members of the 8th Battalion swarmed out to give the females of the city their biggest treat.

Harold Buddenbohm, Kenny Carlon and I set off together. I had forgiven Kenny for his indiscretion in the boxing ring.

Riding the cable cars and trudging the hilly streets of San Francisco soon wore us out, so we decided to go to a movie. Finding one, we stood in line before the box-office amid dozens of soldiers, sailors and Marines. Even some foreign allied servicemen were there in line, too. We also noticed that servicemen received a discount when purchasing a ticket. We could use all the discount we could get, since an Aviation Cadet's pay of twenty-one dollars a month didn't go very far.

The girl in the ticket office was nonplused. Since we wore no insignia, she could not determine whether or not we were really servicemen. If we were not, we would have to pay full price for the tickets, which we could ill afford to do.

Finally, still in a quandary, she asked what branch of the service we were in. Being first in line, I said, "Ve are Roosian commandos." Both Bood and Ken took up the play-acting with, "Yah, yah, ve be Rooshian commandos, yust out vrom Stalingrad. Yah, yah." With that we all three started to jabber in what we imagined Russian sounded like, with lots of gestures.

In order to speed things up, she gave us our tickets, with the servicemen's discount, and we went inside to see the movie.

THANKSGIVING 1942

According to the records of the battalion, we were all in better shape by the first of November than we had been when we entered pre-flight in September. Lt. Boscetti showed us how much faster we completed the agility course, how we were able to do more push-ups and chinnings and myriad other improvements in our physical being.

I guess he was right. But I think he was wrong when he rated Bood.

Toward the end of our training at St. Mary's, Bood and I were assigned to military track as our primary athletic event.

Military track is a polite name for the obstacle course. The course at St. Mary's consisted of a series of barriers, fences, mud holes, water jumps, walls, trees, swings, ladders and nets, all of which had to be overcome as we raced against the clock.

I never did complete a full lap of the course. Neither did Bood. He had more difficulty than I. When I came to an obstacle my tired body could not surmount, I proceeded to go around it and move on to the next barrier. Bood had a more determined approach, but the wall barriers were his nemesis.

One afternoon Bood and I were out on the course. Both of us had successfully negotiated the water jump, the mudholes and swings. The next obstacle was the six-foot wall we were to vault or climb over.

I walked around it, and watched Bood.

Backing off about fifty feet, Bood raced toward the wall. Faster and faster he went. Then, instead of even making even a slight attempt to leap or vault the wall, he ran full tilt into it! The sound of flesh hitting a wooden wall echoed over the track. *Splat!*

Bood staggered, pulled himself together, backed off a few feet and charged once more at the wall.

Kerthud! His body hit the unyielding barricade. Bood recoiled a bit, gathered himself once more and charged at the pesky wall. Once more he flattened himself against the wooden structure. Two more times the persistent Buddenbohm attacked the wall, and two more times he was halted. He made no attempt to use his arms to assist in scaling the barricade. When I finally stopped him before the wall, I asked him how come he kept running into the thing without trying to go around it like I did.

"Jus' wanna get past that wall; jus' wanna get past the wall. Muh arms are too tired to lift. Gotta get over the wall," he kept repeating.

Lt. Boscetti, watching Bood's performance from afar, finally put himself between Bood and the wall, and called a halt to Bood's fixation on self-destruction.

Eventually the mayhem brought on by pre-flight school came to an end. Our uniforms came, we had increased in strength, we could march and we had become familiar with Navy regulations and basic aeronautical wisdom.

On the day before Thanksgiving, 1942, the 8th Battalion graduated from St. Mary's Pre-Flight School and we scattered out to Primary flight schools across the nation. I was assigned Norman, Oklahoma, as my flight training base.

Given two weeks leave, we all headed for our respective homes. Ten zillion other servicemen also headed for their homes along with the 8th Battalion of Naval Aviation Cadets, and on the same train out of San Francisco. Considering myself fortunate just to be on the train headed for Nebraska, I didn't care one bit that I had no seat or berth assigned me. From California to Salt Lake City I sat on my suitcase in the passageway opposite the ladies' head. I think every female on that train suffered from some sort of bladder disorder. They sure kept me busy getting out of their way. My Thanksgiving dinner was a cheese sandwich supplied by the Red Cross ladies at one of our stops.

NAS NORMAN

At last we were near some airplanes. As we clambered off the bus, we could hear the roar and sputter of aircraft engines, while overhead myriad yellow biplanes seemed to welcome us to Primary flight training at Norman, Oklahoma.

The Primary bases are more commonly known as "E-bases," the "E" standing for "Elimination." While it was remotely possible for a Cadet to wash out at pre-flight school, very few did; it was in Primary that the wheat was separated from the chaff. According to Navy statistics, about 15 percent of the Cadets entering Primary flight training fail to qualify and go instead into other branches of the service. We were told that two thirds of our time at Norman would be spent flying, and the rest would be devoted to physical conditioning and a continuation of the courses we had started in pre-flight—aerology, navigation, communications, engines, recognition, gunnery, etc.

We had started to become military at St. Mary's; at Norman we became even more so. We drilled to the cadence of the "Hup-2-3-4" of our platoon leaders, and learned to keep our hands out of our pockets. We made square corners, and responded to orders with an "Aye, aye, Sir." Walls had become bulkheads, ceilings had changed to overheads, stairs had become ladders, and floors decks. Windows became portholes.

I discovered that the Navy cared little for previous flight experience. Even though I had soloed Cubs with Andy Risser, Aeroncas in CPT at Wayne and Wacos in advanced Civilian Pilot Training at Sioux City, the Navy was unimpressed. When it came time to fly, the Navy acted as though none of us had ever seen a flying machine. This in spite of the fact that many of the CPT graduates had been sponsored by the Navy.

No sooner had we disembarked from the gray Navy bus than an officer came out of the administration building, ordered us to "fall in," and marched us across the street to an athletic field. We were all in our dress blues! Even though we were not in our athletic gear, he required us all to run the "agility course," a track with wooden blocks scattered along the route near containers. We were required to dash along the track, pick up the articles and put them in the boxes, then speed to the next group of objects and do the same thing with them. Sometimes we were required to take the blocks out of the box and line them up on the track. It was supposed to improve our dexterity, and I guess it did, but it wasn't easy to do in black dress shoes, dress uniforms and white shirts with starched collars.

At long last, after having been Aviation Cadets since September, we were finally introduced to the planes we were to train on, the ubiquitous "Yellow Peril," the Stearman N2S. Powered with either a 220- or 225-horsepower Lycoming or Jacobs engine, they were in the same category as the UPF-7s we had flown in Secondary CPT. They had taller landing gear that seemed to have a narrower wheel base than the Wacos, and we wondered if they were prone to ground loop.

Prior to our first flights, we were assigned by the Flight Department to our instructors. There were three Cadets to each instructor; Ensign Hayward was to be my instructor.

Hayward had been a civilian flight instructor in Texas, and had been taken into the Navy through one of their programs. Unlike some of the other instructors, Ensign Hayward cared little for military protocol and dress. It struck me as odd that he always wore cowboy boots when he flew. Maybe with his Texas background, he considered the Stearman to be an aerial pinto horse.

After successfully passing the oral and written test on the Stearman, on December 8, 1942, I had my first official flight as an Aviation Cadet with Ensign Hayward in Stearman N2S Bureau No. 07070.

My career as a Naval Aviator had begun.

SOLO

Above the roar of the Lycoming engine I could plainly hear Ensign Lewis hollering. He was definitely upset with me.

I was in the process of demonstrating my version of a power landing, with obviously disastrous results. Ensign Lewis was my check pilot, and was seated in the front cockpit of the galloping Stearman. It was up to him to determine if I could deftly take off and land the Navy trainer without making an undue spectacle of myself.

I had been instructed to make a power landing when we returned to the main base. Ensign Lewis seemed at ease with my ability to handle the "Yellow Peril," and he assumed my landing at the conclusion of the check ride would be of little interest or hazard.

How wrong he was.

Using too much power and far too much speed, I flew the Stearman into the runway with a *kerplongg!* At once the plane leaped into the air, to return a few yards further down the runway with another bone-jarring jolt, then high into the air it went, "porpoising" down the runway, with a shaken student pilot (me) trying to regain control.

Unable to stand the bouncing flight any longer, Ensign Lewis sprang into action. Directing a few well-chosen phrases toward what he considered my doubtful parentage, he wrenched the controls from me and brought an end to the galloping landing. From his caustic remarks concerning my piloting ability, I assumed that I would be given a "down" for my check ride.

My assumption was correct. I was.

This happened the week before Christmas, and it was obvious my Christmas was to be ruined by the Navy.

In 1942, if a student pilot failed to pass his flight check, he was given three opportunities to mend his ways before being "washed out." A quaking Aviation Cadet, I was summoned before the squadron officers to determine if I were worthy of receiving extra instruction, so that hopefully I could be taught to bring the aircraft safely back to the ground without making a spectacle of myself.

My instructor, Ensign Hayward, stood by me. Using logic that would have done Clarence Darrow proud, he argued my case. He assured the board that I was not a kamikaze pilot in western guise, and that, contrary to the rumors that were being bandied about, there was no proof that I was in the hire of the Luftwaffe. He allowed that, with a bit more instruction, I could be taught to make a Navy-approved power landing without making a fool of him or the Navy.

The wash-out board took pity on me and gave me the extra time in which to shape up. Ensign Hayward was the epitome of patience as he coaxed me through the landings, and at last the technique came to me. I was ready for flight check number two.

My second attempt was scheduled for Christmas day. A wary Lt. Keahey was to be my check pilot. That day I couldn't miss. The wheel landings, which had caused me so much trouble, came off without a hitch. Finally, Lt. Keahey told me to land and pull off the runway. He got out of the plane, patted me on the shoulder and told me to go up and make three landings.

Which I did.

That day, an exuberant Navy Aviation Cadet, V-5, USNR, sent a telegram home which read, "Soloed today. Best Christmas present ever. Bob."

The author in his first airplane in August 1928. Named *The Spirit of St. Vitis,* the craft was built of laths covered with canvas from his brother's pup tent. The author is wearing an aviator's helmet, popular attire for the late '20s.

The "head" at Agadir. The perimeter fence is near the trees in the background. It is here the author prepared for an attack by what he feared were marauding natives.

Graduation picture of Jack Curran, taken in 1936 at Sacred Heart School, Norfolk, Nebraska.

Aerial view of Rickenbacker Field, Stevens, South Dakota, where Advanced CPT flight training was given by Morningside College, Sioux City, Iowa. Graham Flying Service was the contractor. J-3 Cubs are seen lined up in the area across from the hangars. One Waco UPF-7 can be seen at the end of one row of J-3s.

The author in the cockpit of a Waco UPF-7, ready for take-off.

The author and Ensign H.I. Adelt with model Spitfire built while awaiting orders at Norfolk, Virginia, in fall, 1943.

Civil Pilot Training

MORNINGSIDE COLLEGE ⇔ GRAHAM FLYING SERVICE

This Is To Certify: That *Robert Lynn Carlisle* has satisfactorily completed the

Secondary Course

GROUND
(240 Hours)

Code
Theory of Flight and Aircraft
Aircraft Engine Operation
Aircraft Identification
Military Forces Organization
Military and Physical Training

FLIGHT
(40 Hours)

Navigation
Meteorology

Taxiing
Takeoffs
Traffic Pattern
Straight and Level
Rectangular Course
S Turns Across a Road

Series of Eights
Pylon Eights
Climbing Turns
Series of Turns
Steep Turns
Chandelles

Lazy Eights
Series of Stalls
Spins
Forward Slip
Spiral

Glides and Glide Turns
Accuracy Landings
Emergencies
Loop

Immelman
Slow Roll
Snap Roll
Vertical Reversements
Half Roll

Issued this *fifth* day of *Sept.*, 1942

W. E. Graber, GROUND SCHOOL
E. R. Graham, FLIGHT SCHOOL

Certificate given to author upon completion of CPT Course in aerobatics at Morningside College, Sioux City, Iowa.

Author as an Aviation Cadet in his dress blues at Seal Rock, San Francisco, California.

Marine "boondockers" worn by the author's Cadet battalion on their first liberty at St. Mary's Pre-Flight School, Moraga, California

View of another PBY from the port blister, location of one of the 50-caliber waist guns. A similar blister and gun were on the starboard side.

PBY on patrol over the Atlantic, taken from another P-boat. The author is flying this plane and is being relieved from convoy coverage.

Approaching Ascension Island after the flight from Natal, Brazil. The airstrip blasted out of the volcanic rock is on the other side of the island.

The only tree on Ascension Island, located on the Commanding Officer's compound.

Agadir, French Morocco. An old Portuguese fort overlooks the town, with the bay and town below. The Air France airfield is located to the far right of the picture.

VP-73's base at Agadir, French Morocco. The PBY-5A patrol planes can be seen in the distance.

Squadron insignia of Patrol-Bombing Squadron 73. During peacetime, in the area below the red Indian was painted "VP-73." For security reasons the squadron number was removed during wartime.

Lt. (jg.) Robert J. Fuchs's PBY burns after crashing on take-off from Agadir. All members of the flight crew were killed. The squadron's tents can be seen in the background.

(Left) Rest and relaxation: Lt. Vyrl E. Leichliter pitching horseshoes at Agadir, French Morocco.
(Above) Lt. (jg.) Robert L. Carlisle (left) and his flying mate, Lt. (jg.) Oren W. Marshall at Agadir, French Morocco.

Our Executive Officer, Lt. Dwight Hundley. At the end of the street is the Officers Club. Agadir, French Morocco, November, 1943.

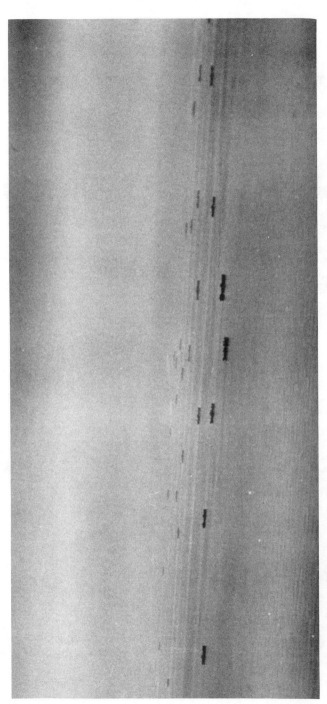

Atlantic convoy, 1943. At times the convoy would reach from horizon to horizon. Since they could move only as fast as the slowest ship, the convoys offered an intriguing target to German U-boats. VP-73 never lost a ship that it was escorting due to enemy action.

VP-73 Catalina on patrol over the Atlantic. Note how the haze has blurred the horizon.

Coach William (Bear) Bryant as a Lieutenant attached to the Headquarters Squadron (Hedron) at Port Lyautey, French Morocco. Later he became famous as the head coach at the University of Alabama.

Commandante Paul Le Conde of the Free French Armée de l'Air, whom we flew to Gilbraltar.

Ensign Daniel Perch and his bride, at the time of their marriage at 90 Church Street in New York City.

Air France control tower at Port Lyautey. It was camouflaged with irregular patches of light green paint.

Practice bombing of a float light. Only one bomb was released (two were intended). The white plume in the smoke of the float light is the bomb burst. Had both bombs released, this would have been considered a straddle (i.e., a hit). The wing tip of the photographing OS2U is clearly shown.

VP-73 Catalina in flight, setting out for anti-submarine sweep off Gibraltar. The PBYs were painted white, with the upper side of the wings and stabilizers dark sea-gray.

The author deep in thought, Floyd Bennett Field, 1944.

Officers and men of Patrol Squadron 73 mustered for inspection, spring, 1944. The author is in the second row, under the arrow.

U-235 surrendering off Cape May, New Jersey, on May 7, 1945. An American Destroyer Escort (DE) is at the right.

The author (left) and Lt. (jg.) Arthur N. Smith in San Juan, Puerto Rico, 1944.

Part IV: Reaching The Goal

10 July 1942—Allies invade Sicily.

17 August 1942—Sicilian campaign terminated; Lipari and Stromboli Islands surrender to U.S. destroyers and PT boats.

12 November 1943—73-P-11 encounters two German Focke-Wulf 200Cs over the convoy they are covering. By staying above the convoy and flying head-on toward the attacking bombers, the convoy, with the exception of one ship, is saved. Three members of the flight crew are wounded by enemy gunfire.

26 December 1943—The squadron starts on the return trip to the USA via Agadir, Ruisque (Dakar), Roberts Field (Liberia), Ascension Island, Natal, Belém (Brazil), Trinidad, B.W.I., San Juan, Puerto Rico and Jacksonville, Florida.

NIGHT FLIGHT

For almost a month after my solo flight, the Navy kept me busy learning the fundamentals of military flying. Day after day we flew in the winter sky over the red dust of Oklahoma. On many occasions we Cadets flew twice a day. In the morning an instructor taught us aerobatics; in the afternoon we flew solo to further sharpen our skills at loops, slow rolls, Immelmanns, snap rolls, split-Esses and all of the maneuvers thought necessary to survive in combat. The Stearman seemed a better aerobatic ship than the Waco UPF-7s of Secondary CPT.

Toward the end of January we reached the part of the flying syllabus that called for night flying. Since none of us had ever flown at night, we looked forward to this training with some apprehension.

My night flying instructor was Ensign Fuqua.

Early in the evening of January 22, the Cadets scheduled for night flying met with their instructors while the Chief of Flight, Lt. John, briefed the group on the procedures to be followed. By half an hour before sundown our Stearmans had been pre-flighted and we took off, one by one, to circle the main field. We climbed, circled, glided and landed, then took off again to repeat the take-offs and landings as darkness enveloped the land. There were twelve of us in all. According to the procedure outlined in the briefing, we flew in line astern, with about a thousand feet separating each plane.

The landing area was marked by four flare pots, the black, round bomb-like type used by highway departments to mark obstructions. We were to land to the right of the flares, as close to them as possible.

For the first hour, with our instructors aboard, the night flying went smoothly. For at least half of that time we flew in fading light, and we had no difficulty at all either following the ships ahead or landing near the flare pots.

When the first period came to an end, we each landed and taxied back to the line, where our instructors got out of the planes. We were then waved back to the take-off spot, and one by one we took off in single file, the plane behind following the white navigation light on the tail of the one ahead. It was now pitch dark.

It was then that things became SNAFU (Situation Normal All Fouled Up).

One of the lead planes, evidently by mistake, followed a star, or perhaps the flickering lights of the Norman to Oklahoma City streetcar, and elongated the circle in the traffic pattern. Soon planes were flying every which way, with no set pattern. At one time I spotted the red and green wing-tip lights of another Stearman headed directly for me!

I pulled up, banked over and looked down into the dimly lit cockpit of a fellow Cadet's plane. He missed me!

Convinced that discretion was the better part of valor, I added power and headed up and away from the melee of Stearmans. I finally throttled back some distance away from the swarm of night-fliers and circled near Oklahoma City, watching the twisting red, green and white lights over the base. Finally, no more planes appeared to be orbiting the field, and I cautiously returned to the airport. I landed without any trouble, the last one in.

I was immediately taken to the operations office, where the Chief of Flight had the eleven other Cadets squirming. "Boys," he boomed, "if you want to kill yourselves, just keep that up." He proceeded to tongue lash us fore and aft for our dismal performance. "Now," he said, "go up and do that business right."

We did.

FLYING ACES

Following our misadventure in night flying, a rather subdued class of Aviation Cadets began their indoctrination in a new phase of military aviation: formation flying.

In addition to the regular ground school courses in Morse code, D.R. navigation, celestial navigation, power plants, aircraft and ship recognition, aircraft instruments, aerial gunnery, Navy regulations, aerodynamics, aviation mathematics and physics, aerology and communications, a new subject was added: hand signals to be used in formation flying.

Because the Stearmans were not equipped with radios, the Navy, through years of research, had developed a series of hand movements to be used by the formation leader to signal pertinent orders to other members of the flight. These signals were: right echelon—right arm raised; left echelon—left arm raised; right turn—right thumb motion to right (like thumbing a ride); left turn—left thumb motion to left; climb—point up; descend—point down; speed up—flat of hand, pushing forward; reduce speed—rotate fist as though lowering flaps; break up formation—raise hand and rotate in circle; assume lead—pat top of head and point to other ship who is to lead. Finally, the signal for execution is when the hand comes down.

At night before "lights out" we practiced the signals faithfully from one top bunk to the other. We had them down pat.

All of the flights we had made in the Stearmans up to this point had been done from the rear seat. In formation flying, we would fly from the front seat, and we were given special dual instruction by our instructors for this change in seating.

Once we had flown from the front cockpit we could understand how our flight instructors could be aloft with their students, one after the other, without succumbing to the bitter cold to which the students in the rear cockpits were subjected. There was absolutely no blast from the slipstream in the front cockpit, and it was so still you could have lit a cigarette. During the flight, the icy blast from the propeller was deflected upward by the windshield to the underside of the center section of the wing, where it was diverted back down into the rear cockpit holding the frozen Cadet. And the winter air in Oklahoma was on the sub-polar side. But immediately behind the Lycoming engine, the heat almost caused our flying boots to melt.

Prior to the formation flying training, all of us cringed when we saw other Stearmans within a half mile of our planes. Now, it seemed, we couldn't get close enough. We flew for miles over the Oklahoma countryside with our wings just a few feet from each other. Right and left echelons, line abreast and finger-fours were among the formations we mastered.

Most of the formations were made up of five-plane sections. Assignment of flight leader was made by the flight department and was rotated among all members of the flight. Many times we switched lead during the flight by using the proper signal.

This was one time, when, as Aviation Cadets, we all felt as though we were pilots on a par with those we had seen in movies of the late 1920s and '30s—*Dawn Patrol* and *Hell's Angels*. Through one bit of trickery or another, we all obtained colorful scarves or stockings from female admirers and tied them to the backs of our helmets, where they streamed in the wind, making us look like Errol Flynn or Richard Dix, we thought. I wore a red scarf tied to my helmet.

On February 15, as a graduation exercise, we flew a fifteen-plane formation over the Naval Air Station as a farewell to Norman and Oklahoma City. Our next stop would be advanced training at Corpus Christi Naval Air Station, Texas.

CORPUS

An exuberant group of Naval Aviation Cadets piled into the bus that was to take them to the railroad station. No sooner had the bus driver closed the doors than one of them began leading the Cadets in a popular song of the day: "The stars at night are deep and bright *(clap—clap—clap)* deep in the heart of Texas," went the lyric, over and over again. Occasionally the song leader would suggest a new song. The most popular ones were "Pistol Packin' Mama" and "Don't Fence Me In." We were getting in a Texas frame of mind.

Arriving at the Naval Air Training Center early in the afternoon, we were met by a fleet of gray Navy buses and taken to "Mainside." Here we were processed by a swarm of yeomen.

REACHING THE GOAL

[handwritten: My Basic Base, Squadron & Type Plane]

Finally, with everything seemingly in order, we were again directed to the buses and were taken to the many outlying fields surrounding the main facility. I was assigned to Squadron 12-A, based at Cuddihy Field. We were to fly Vultee SNV-1s. *[handwritten: 1st flying]*

The Vultee Valiant was a low-wing monoplane with a 450-horsepower Pratt and Whitney Wasp-Junior radial engine. It was equipped with a full instrument panel for all-weather flying, flaps and controllable pitch propeller, and was very similar to the operational planes of the Fleet. The instructor occupied the rear cockpit, while the student flew from the front. When instrument training was to be given, the Cadet sat in the aft position.

Once more we started from the bottom and began taking dual instruction in the Vultees. This time, however, it seemed as though our progress was much more rapid. On March 29, I had my first flight in the SNV, and I soloed in one on the 1st of April!

After about ten hours of solo flight time we began formation flying. The routine was much the same as at Primary, only now we became proficient in making cross-overs, step-ups and step-down "V" formations and echelons, and toward the end of the formation flights, we were making formation take-offs.

Upon completing this stage we were transferred to the outlying Cabaniss Field to Squadron 12-D, where we began instrument training. It was here we were introduced to the Link trainer.

The Link was a non-flying copy of the cockpit of an airplane. Once in the machine, a cover was put over the operator so that he could not see out, and using the controls and instruments of the Link he simulated actual flight without ever leaving the ground. The flight was traced on the instructor's desk so that its path could be recorded.

It was in the Link trainer department that we had our first contact with the women of the Navy, the WAVEs. Most of the Link instructors were WAVEs, and they knew what they were up to. Many of them were ex-school teachers and knew how to handle capricious students. Woebetide a Cadet who tried to flirt or make time with his WAVE instructor! During his next Link session he was apt to find himself pitched hither and yon as she turned on "rough air" or caused the radio beam to fade as he was on his final approach to the station. They knew how to handle any Lothario who turned up.

When not in the Links, we were in the rear cockpits of the Vultees, our outside vision blocked by a canvas hood, flying the radio range, bringing the ships out of "unusual positions" and learning to handle an aircraft by depending solely on the instruments with no outside reference points. It became almost like a game, both in the Link and in the SNV, like a game in an arcade. Only in this game the stakes were much higher.

DECISIONS, DECISIONS

As our instrument course in Squadron 12D neared its conclusion, all of us were faced with making two very important decisions.

The first was to decide what type of plane we wished to fly—fighter, torpedo bomber, observation scout, dive bomber or patrol bomber—or whether to become an instructor.

The other decision to be made was whether to become an officer and pilot in the Naval Reserve or in the Marine Corps Reserve.

A combination of personal preference and instructor's recommendations were the main factors governing the types of planes we would fly. I thought the matter over completely and decided that I would like to fly the patrol bombers. Although I had successfully completed all of the syllabus in the aerobatic portions of the flight training, I didn't like that kind of flying as much as some of the Cadets did. Further, since I would be a Navy pilot, it was natural to assume that flying over water would occupy most of my flying time; therefore I thought a flying boat or seaplane would be handy to fly. Then too, the big seaplanes carried more equipment, bombs, guns and survival gear than the smaller planes. Instrument flying caused me no problems, and I assumed that the long-range patrol planes would be flying on instruments much of the time. The final reason for my decision was that multi-engine flight time would be of more value to me should I decide to fly with an airline after the war. Not many single-engine ships were used to fly passengers and cargo.

My instructors agreed with my selection of the VP squadron, and when the assignments were made known, I was one of the few who did not protest the designation of patrol bomber pilot. That was one decision out of the way. Joe Foss helped with the other.

Potential Navy and Marine Corps aviators received the same flight training up to the time they completed their advanced syllabus. Upon finishing the instrument course of Squadron 12D each Cadet was given the opportunity either to stay in the Navy or become a Marine.

As we neared the end of our flights in the instrument-laden SNVs, the Public Relations Department helped us make that decision.

Major Joe Foss, USMC, holder of the Congressional Medal of Honor, was touring Naval and Marine Corps bases throughout the country. Foss, who shot down twenty-six Japanese planes over Guadalcanal, was scheduled to address the Cadets at NAS Corpus Christi on a hot, humid day in early May. Cadet regiments from all of the outlying bases were bussed to the Primary athletic field for the event. There must have been several hundred khaki-clad Cadets drawn up in tight formation all over the field. A raised platform commonly used by the athletic instructors was the speaker's stage.

Because Major Foss was a Medal of Honor holder, we were called to attention as he mounted the platform. For what seemed like three hours (though it probably was no longer than thirty minutes) the Marine Corps Ace of Aces extolled the glories of the Corps. On and on he went as we sweltered in the hot Texas sun. Cadets by the dozen, having locked their knees standing at attention, keeled over with a moan. Corpsmen ran hither and yon giving succor to them. At long last, the oratory came to an end, the speaker climbed down from the platform, and we were marched off the field. Each one of us resolved to never become a Marine. We'd had it! The Marine Corps lost more pilots that day than they ever did in the fighting over Guadalcanal or elsewhere in the South Pacific. When my class of one hundred eighty graduated on July

10, 1943, only thirty-one became members of the Corps, the fewest of any class that year. Major Joe Foss helped make those decisions, he and a hot Texas sun.

SQUADRON 18

I was well pleased with my last two check rides in the SNV. My check pilot, Ensign Lewellen, noted in my log book, "Instrument X—O.K. Radio X—O.K."

We had been up flying instruments and using the low-frequency radio range, the one using the "A" and "N" signals. The check ride fiasco of Christmas week of 1942 was not repeated. I was ready for the patrol bombers I had requested to fly.

Based at Mainside, Squadron 18 flew PBY-3 Consolidated Catalina patrol planes. These had no landing gear; rather, they were flying boats that required beaching gear to be attached in order to drag them up the ramp onto the parking area. The PBYs were twin-engine planes that carried a crew of nine. They had a wing-span of 104 feet and were among the largest planes in the Navy.

Three Cadets went along on each flight, alternating their flight duties during the three- to four-hour training mission. The two who were not up in the cockpit with the instructor learned about the duties of the plane captain, radioman and aerial gunner from the enlisted men in the flight crew. As time went on, the Cadets, under the watchful eyes of their mentors, manned the engineer's position in the "tower," the radioman's earphones and typewriter and the fifty-caliber machine guns in the blisters aft.

A water take-off in a PBY was a production. Once the craft was slowly lowered down the sloping ramp into the water, the beaching crew waded out to the ship, neck-deep in the water, and detached the auxiliary wheels and floated them to a position near the shore. The engines had already been started just prior to entering the water, and once free of the beaching gear, the plane was

REACHING THE GOAL

taxied out to the take-off position marked by buoys. The engines were run up and checked during the taxiing.

For a few moments we held our position with the engines idling, allowing the plane to weathercock into the wind. When the plane's bow pointed into the wind and all stations had reported ready for take-off, both pilot and co-pilot braced themselves on the rudder pedals and pulled the yoke back as far as they could and held it, giving full up elevator. The pilot, in the left seat, held the yoke with his left arm and hand and used his right to push the throttles, mounted overhead, full forward.

The engine roared, the bow reared up and the PBY plowed through the waves, water cascading over the wings and into the propellers. Finally, having gained some speed, the nose dropped, the ship rode on the step, speed was gained and the plane could lift off.

Once the plane was on the step and planing over the water, control over the ailerons and rudder was obtained. After about a mile of being the "fastest boat in the harbor," the plane could be brought off the water and into the air with a slight back pressure. The wing-tip floats were raised and further speed was gained, and the Catalina climbed majestically away.

The mention of speed was only relative. We took off at 80 knots, climbed at 80 knots, cruised at 80 knots, and glided at 80 knots.

We were taught the art of water landings, which required much more skill than the take-offs. Most of the time we made power landings, flying the ship down to just a few feet from the surface, letting down little by little until contact was made, then reducing power and sloshing to a halt. If too much speed was maintained, the plane skipped into the air to return with a splash, and porpoised again and again until speed was reduced and control regained. Some of our early landings were so rough that rivets were popped from the hull, causing the plane captain to dig into his stock of sharpened pencils, which he jammed into the hole to stop the seepage.

We had a lot to learn, but we were on our way to becoming P-boat pilots.

PREMONITION

Several weeks before graduation I received a disturbing letter from home. Mother had received a telephone call from the mother of Brooks ——. Mrs. —— told her that Brooks had a great fear of getting killed, and she, Mrs. ——, wanted to know if I had ever expressed that fear.

I had never considered it, and Mother told her so.

Brooks was a few weeks behind me at Corpus and had asked for—and been assigned to—torpedo bombers, the TBF, Grumman Avenger.

Until I heard about this from home, I didn't know Brooks was at Corpus. It took a bit of doing, but I finally located him at the outlying Waldron Field.

Receiving permission to leave the main base, I took the station bus to Waldron so I could speak to him as his mother had requested. I found him in his room, sitting, staring at the wall.

When he saw me standing in the doorway, he seemed genuinely glad to see me, and we kidded a bit about the last time I'd seen him in Norfolk after CPT in Sioux City, when he had been sporting all of those wings on his uniform. He seemed in a good mood at first, then he asked me to sit down, and said he had to talk to me.

"I'm going to get killed," he began. "I've been assigned TBFs, and I'm going to get killed."

"For Pete's sake," I said, "if you think you're going to be like Torpedo Squadron 8, forget it. The TBF is a heck of a lot better plane than the TBDs that Ensign Gay flew. Besides," I added, "if you feel that way, why don't you talk to your instructor and tell him, or go talk to the chaplain?"

"No," he said. "If I talk to them and tell them how I feel, they'll ground me, and I won't get my wings."

"Well, if that's the case," I said, "why don't you ask for something other than the TBF? Tell them you would rather fly an OS2U or a PBY, or you'd rather be an instructor. They'd listen. The Navy doesn't want a guy with your attitude flying around. Tell them you want to fly a different kind of a plane for the good of the Navy. That always gets them."

Brooks adamantly refused to seek any advice from anyone. Nothing I could say caused him to change his mind. Getting his Wings of Gold was uppermost in his mind—that and getting killed.

As I left him, I asked him to quit writing his folks about his fears, as they had enough to fret about, and to be a little more cheery when he wrote to them. "We should do all we can to help the homefront," I said, trying to joke about things.

He promised he would.

Upon being commissioned and receiving his wings, Brooks was assigned a torpedo squadron in Seattle, Washington. Shortly after his arrival, on a familiarization flight in a TBF, Brooks struck a mountain while making a practice run. He and his two crew members were killed.

Brooks was already dead when I talked to him at Corpus. I'm sure of that.

LT. LESGALIER

One of the most difficult parts of seaplane flying had nothing to do with flying, but took place when the ship was safely on the water with both engines idling. It was called "making the buoy."

Since we were flying PBY-3s in Squadron 18, we were required to conduct water maneuvering constantly. The Catalinas had to be taxied up to the buoys anchored adjacent to the take-off sealanes prior to being hauled up the ramps once the beaching gear was attached. This required knowledge of the wind, current and the sailing ability of the pilot in order to be accomplished with some show of seamanship.

It was during this taxiing practice that I tangled with Lt. Lesgalier.

Lt. Lesgalier had served as an Officer-in-Command of an armed guard of a merchant ship early in the war. This was a crew of six to eight Navy ratings who manned a five-inch gun, usually mounted on the stern of a merchant ship to defend it against enemy raiders or submarines. Upon transferring from the armed guard to flight training, he eventually arrived at NAS Corpus Christi and Squadron 18.

As an officer training with Aviation Cadets, Lt. Lesgalier had the world by the tail. He lived in the BOQ (Bachelor Officers Quarters), had access to the Officers' Club, no restrictions on his liberty, and drew a full Lieutenant's pay.

At Squadron 18 he was assigned to my flight instructor, Ensign Keene.

Though Lesgalier out-ranked Keene, at no time was he allowed to pull rank on the instructor. Ensign Keene saw to that. Time and again it was pointed out to the ex-armed guard officer that he was a Cadet like the rest, and his rank carried no weight on the flight line as long as he was in training. That didn't set too good with Lt. Lesgalier, I could see.

After we had been checked out in the PBY-3s, Lt. Lesgalier and I were scheduled for a training flight and a session of practicing mooring procedures.

The flight portion came off pretty well, considering that the Lieutenant regarded himself my instructor in some of the aerial maneuvers we were doing. The trouble came when we started the water-handling procedures.

As I neared the buoy carefully, approaching slowly into the wind with the engines at what I considered the right speed, Lt. Lesgalier grabbed the throttles, added power and spoiled my whole approach. I asked him what he was doing, and he criticized the way I had made the approach. I told him I knew what I was doing, and to keep his hands off the throttle when I was making the approach. I further told him he was a Cadet, as far as I was concerned, and didn't know any more about making a buoy than I.

Calling him a Cadet didn't sit too well, I could plainly see.

Once more I tried to approach the buoy, and sure enough, just as I got close enough for the crewman in the bow to hook the pendant with a boathook, Lesgalier once more took over the throttles and caused me to get out of position and miss the mooring. Highly indignant, to put it mildly, I took my hands off the control wheel and throttle, took my feet off the rudder pedals, and said, "Okay, mate, you do it."

Lt. Lesgalier began hollering at me for my insubordination, and ended his tirade with, "I command you to do as I say, and I'm putting you on report!"

Being put on report was a serious matter.

I gave the irate Lieutenant only the assistance needed to get the PBY hauled up on the beach. I went directly to my instructor and asked him to meet me in the flight office. I explained my problem, that I did not consider Lt. Lesgalier my superior while on the flight line and while learning to fly. To me, he was a Cadet, regardless of his two stripes. The instructor agreed with me, and transferred Lt. Lesgalier to another crew. I had no further difficulty in water-handling a PBY.

FDR

For several days the radio news broadcasts told of a coming meeting of President Roosevelt and President Comacho of Mexico. The accounts also hinted that the conferences would be held at an as-yet-unnamed military base.

When I heard this report, I told my roommate, "I bet Roosevelt is coming to Corpus." He scoffed, but I held my ground.

One morning, shortly after hearing this announcement, we woke up to find armed sailors on every rooftop, patrolling the streets and all areas of the base. Obviously something was up.

Suddenly the P.A. system blared: "Now Hear This! Now Hear This! All Cadets fall out at 1100 in Class A uniforms. All duties are suspended while you all police the area fore and aft. That is all!"

Suddenly the Officer of the Deck was bustling around shouting orders and directing one and all to "bear a hand," giving us naval commands more fit to be used on a man-o'-war than on policing a barracks.

Eleven hundred found the entire Cadet regiment mustering before their respective barracks, undergoing roll call and inspection. When the regimental officers considered us properly dressed, our Cadet platoon leaders were instructed to march us off to the inspection area, wherever that was.

We were marched several blocks, with the Cadet officers calling cadence, and finally arrived at the main avenue of the base. We were drawn up on the parking near the curbs, given an "at ease," and told to wait.

By now we had been told that our visitor would be President Roosevelt.

Cadets by the thousands lined the avenue, having been bussed in from all of the outlying fields for the event.

As we stood on the curbs waiting, several officers passed up and down the ranks asking for Cadets to volunteer to box, wrestle and run the obstacle course for the President. Those who volunteered were sent to their barracks to put on their gym gear and go to the athletic field.

I was standing in the second rank facing the avenue. Directly in front of me was a Cadet from Sioux City, Iowa, Fred Davenport. Fred had been in Secondary CPT with me. He was a big fellow, six feet tall, and he must have weighed 250 pounds. As he stood before me, I was unable to see around him, and I knew when President Roosevelt came, I'd have no glimpse of him.

"Hey, Fred," I said to him, "how about changing places with me? You're a Republican of the worse kind, and you don't care if you ever see Roosevelt. How about changing places with me, so a good Democrat can see his leader?"

With little protest from Fred, we changed places.

All at once, from far down the street, we could hear the various formations being called to "Tens-hut!" Soon we, too, responded to the command.

In a few moments the motorcade came down the street flanked by secret service men and motorcyclists. In the lead was the limousine bearing the President and Comacho. FDR was wearing a white Panama hat and a white suit. He smiled and waved to the Cadets on review. In the car behind were Mrs. Roosevelt and Mrs.

Comacho. They, too, waved. A third limousine completed the procession. It contained six dark-haired ladies. "Those are Comacho's concubines," said a Cadet beside me.

As the motorcade passed the athletic fields, it slowed down to enable the guests to view the struggling Cadets, manfully performing for their Commander-in-Chief. Moving on, the limousines drew up along the seawall to witness a dive-bombing demonstration by a formation of SNJs flown by instructors from Kingsville Field. Their practice bombs missed the target by a mile.

Soon it was all over. The Cadets were marched back to their barracks and the guards disappeared.

But I was happy. I had seen President Roosevelt.

NAV FLIGHT

By the middle of June we were all preparing for our first long overwater navigation flight. We had been practicing bomb- and torpedo-dropping, radio, celestial and dead-reckoning navigation, and we were considered ready for this next step in our flight training.

On June 18, Lt. Hartsook, our navigation instructor, briefed Cadets Jim Cain, Ray Denholm and me on the coming problem. We were to take off at 1300 and fly a triangular course, each leg being two hundred miles in length. Lt. Hartsook designated the latitude and longitude at which to change course, which we marked on the chart of the Gulf of Mexico, over which we were to fly. He also pointed out that, since German U-boats had done some damage to shipping in the Gulf, we would be flying a fully armed PBY, complete with depth charges and ammunition for the 50-caliber guns in the blisters. He informed us we would be flying a PBY5-A for the hop. The 5A, he stated, was an amphibious version of the planes we had been flying, and since it had wheels, we would take off from the runways of the main base rather than from the water. He said he would make the take-off and final landing, but during the rest of the flight we three Cadets would run the mission and he would only step in if we required assistance.

We drew straws to see who would be the first to occupy the cockpit, and Jim Cain was named to be the PPC (Patrol Plane Commander) on the first leg. Ray was to be second, and I was named to fly back to the base.

At 1200 we were at the plane, laden down with our navigation kit containing charts, sextant, the celestial navigation books, the HO-214, the Air Almanac and star charts. By 1245 we had the Catalina pre-flighted and informed Lt. Hartsook that all was shipshape and ready for take-off.

Promptly at 1300, PBY-5A, Bureau No. 08057 lifted from the runway and headed for Point X-Ray, our point of departure in the Gulf. All three of us commented on how much simpler land-based PBY operations were than water.

Laden with four 325-pound depth charges hanging from the wings, it seemed to take forever to get off the ground. Once in the air with the gear up and with the ship trimmed out, Lt. Hartsook turned over the controls and the entire operation to Cadets Cain, Denholm and Carlisle.

While two of the five-man crew stood watch for U-boats at the aft blisters, the radioman aided us with RDF bearings. Ray and I were busy plotting our position, making drift corrections and making out our estimated time of arrival (ETA) at our first course change.

Several times I took a sun-line to determine our ground speed and checked it with radio bearings supplied by our radioman. Ray took drift sights with the pelorus and smoke floats from the tunnel-gun position aft. Arriving at our first course change, Cadet Cain relinquished the controls, and with Cadet Denholm now in command, we set off for the second leg of the triangular course.

We found out that flying the airplane was a minor part of an over-water mission. A careful log of the flight, accurate computations and a knowledge of wind and sea were needed to ensure success.

I was relieved when it came my turn to occupy the cockpit and give the navigation responsibilities over to Jim and Ray.

After more than six hours in the air, we sighted the beacon of the base off our bow. We had navigated so accurately that Lt.

Hartsook found it unnecessary to make even a slight bank to line up with the runway. He congratulated us on a "job well done."

Six hours in the air seemed like a long time, but it was nothing compared to flights we were to make when we joined the operational squadrons.

WINGS OF GOLD

Advanced training at Corpus Christi was nearing its end. On June 28 I made my last flight in a PBY-3 and began final preparation for graduation, scheduled for July 10.

These preparations included oral and written examinations on everything we had been taught since pre-flight school, including Navy Regulations and all of the ground school subjects.

All of this activity, plus the filling out of myriad forms to be sent to the Bureau of Naval Personnel to verify that I had successfully completed the prescribed course leading to a commission and awarding of those Navy Wings of Gold, kept me busy.

It was also rumored that we were restricted to the base until after graduation. The reason for the restriction stemmed from the fact that, prior to being commissioned, while all the paperwork was being submitted, we were not in the Navy; rather we were civilians for those few hours until the papers were completed and returned.

It was said that, during this period of being in limbo, some Cadets, with Navy flight training behind them, went to the representatives of the Royal Air Force and signed up with them, seeking faster advancement and higher rank than that offered by the Navy.

On July 10, 1943, my class stood at attention on the manicured lawn before the administration building at Corpus Christi Naval Air Training Center and received our commissions and gold wings from Rear Admiral Charles P. Mason, USN, Commandant of NATC.

I had finally achieved the goal I had set for myself in 1940 on the day Jack Curran stood in our living room following his graduation.

Though I was an Ensign in the Navy and had those Wings of Gold, I still was not yet ready for the war. I still had operational training at Jacksonville, Florida. At Jax we would fly the type of aircraft we would use with the Fleet, under conditions approximating actual conditions overseas. The finishing touches would be applied during the two months of operational training.

Given two weeks leave prior to reporting to Jacksonville, I headed home to Norfolk, Nebraska.

As the train pulled out of the station, I thought of the words prominently inscribed in the ready room at Cuddihy Field.

It was called, "The Navy Flyer's Creed." It went like this:

- I am a United States Navy Flyer. My countrymen built the best airplane in the world and entrusted it to me. They trained me to fly it. I will use it to the absolute limit of my power.
- With my fellow pilots, air crews and deck crews, my plane and I will do anything necessary to carry out our tremendous responsibilities. I will always remember we are part of an unbeatable combat team—the United States Navy.
- When the going is fast and rough, I will not falter. I will be uncompromising in every blow I strike. I will be humble in victory.
- I am a United States Navy Flyer. I have dedicated myself to my country, with its many millions of all races, colors and creeds. They and their way of life are worthy of my greatest protective effort.
- I ask the help of God in making that effort great enough.

It had been a long hard road, but I finally made it. I was a Navy Flyer.

BOMBSIGHT

The St. Johns River was the blackest river I had ever seen. I was familiar with the tan muddiness of the Missouri, but the St. Johns really stood out. It must have had a bottom of rich black loam. On its banks was located the Operational Training Base of Naval Air Station, Jacksonville, Florida.

In theory, this was the end of the line in our training, and once we completed it we would be assigned a squadron with the Fleet. No longer would we be flying the obsolete PBY-3. Now we would fly the newer PBY-5, still a seaplane, but with more up-to-date armament and equipment than the earlier models.

We were thrilled to find out that we would be using the Norden bombsight, heralded by the Army Air Corps as the most accurate sight in the world. In fact, the Air Corps claimed that they could put a bomb in a pickle barrel from 10000 feet. According to the newsreels and information released, the Air Corps bombardiers carried the bombsight to the planes covered with canvas after getting them out of a guarded security area. No one but the bombardier was allowed to even get close to it, it was so secret.

We learned that the Navy was not as security-conscious when it came to the bombsight. At our first briefing on the use of the Norden, the instructor stressed its use as a "drift sight" to be used in dead-reckoning navigation. Located in the nose of the Catalina and positioned by the bombing window, when used as a drift sight it gave a very accurate indication of the plane's drift caused by the wind. It was never covered as the Air Corps covered theirs.

Even though the PBY had been eliminated as a high-altitude bomber, we were given training in that, anyway.

With four one-hundred-pound practice bombs in racks under the wing, we struggled to get the Catalina up to 10000 feet, the bombing altitude.

Arriving over the target, we circled to determine whether the area was free of other planes, then flew away several miles, then headed back toward the target. Our ordinance man was the first to make a bombing run, mainly to get the gear in proper operation. We were to drop only one bomb at a time rather than in a stick. That way each of us could get an opportunity to make a run in on the target.

Lt. Helfricks was our instructor. Ensign Jim Cain, who was at Corpus and graduated with me, Ensign Jack Snare and I were to be the bombardiers.

After ordinance had made his drop which, incidentally, was nearly a bull's eye, each one of us took turns. After Jim and Jack had made their runs, my turn finally came.

Squatting over the Norden bombsight on my knees in the bow, I squinted through the eyepiece and adjusted the various dials as instructed. The PPC (Patrol Plane Commander, in this case Lt. Helfricks) began the run in, then switched over the operation to the Sperry Automatic Pilot. After the autopilot was engaged, the bombsight was switched into the autopilot, and from then on all operation was automatic. With the arming switch on, I was fascinated as the course of the plane was corrected according to instructions relayed to it by the bombsight. Then, as I curiously watched through the eyepiece, the crosshairs of the sight neared the target, and suddenly it was "bombs away." The one-hundred-pounder raced toward the bull's eye, and a few moments later I saw a puff of white smoke near the center of the target as the practice bomb hit home. It appeared that the Air Corps' confidence in the Norden bombsight was well grounded.

That was one of the few times in operational training we used the bombsight to actually drop bombs. From then on we dropped them by "seaman's eye," with only our visual acuity and timing as our sight.

It seemed a shame to use that obviously expensive piece of equipment merely to see which way the wind was blowing, but we did anyway.

BRANDED

The flying at the Operational Training Base at NAS Jacksonville was intended to acquaint us with life in a squadron overseas, and to subject us to the more warlike activities of naval operations. In keeping with this idea, we spent much of our time in the air firing the guns at towed aerial sleeves or at targets on the water's surface. This practice was done in conjunction with low-altitude bombing runs using a towed spar as the target. For this practice we dropped cast iron bombs that made a flash of light and a puff of smoke upon contact with the water. No bombsight was used; rather, we targeted by seaman's eye. Pressing the "pickle switch" when the pilot estimated the proper time for release in order to get a straddle required a great deal of quick response and accurate range estimation. It is surprising, however, how accurate we became in this type of bombing. Very seldom did we miss getting a straddle on the target, which would have been a lethal hit had the target been an enemy submarine.

In preparation for the aerial gunnery training, the rounds of each of the waist guns had the ends of the bullets dipped in special non-drying paint. Each gun had bullets painted a different color. As the OS2U flew past towing the target sleeve 2,500 feet behind, the gunner on that side opened fire. Each hit on the muslin sleeve was marked by a paint-rimmed hole, telling which gunner had struck the target. The gunners were then graded on the number of holes they had put in the sleeve. During this practice, the pilot not flying (three were carried on each flight) acted as fire controller, assisting the gunners in locating the oncoming target.

I was fire controller on one of these gunnery flights, and as such I was sitting on the jump seat on the bulkhead in the blister, where the 50-caliber waist guns were mounted.

It was hot, even in the air over Jacksonville, and all of us had taken off our shirts and were wearing our tee-shirts for coolness.

I had gotten low on clean tee-shirts, and rather than wear a dirty one, I had borrowed a clean one from my roommate, Ensign Jim Cain.

Ensign Cain was somewhat bigger than I, and as a result his shirt was a bit baggy on me. In fact, the neck opening was so large that it hung like a horsecollar on me, not close-fitting at all.

As I sat on the jump seat waiting for the OS2U to make its pass, I sat leaning over with my elbows on my knees. The neck of my tee-shirt gaped open.

Suddenly the Kingfisher came into view, and I alerted the gunner. He pulled back the bolt and charged the 50-caliber, then swung the gun into firing position. The OS came into view, flew past, and when the cloth sleeve came into range, the gunner opened up.

Brass flew in every direction from the firing. Suddenly I saw one of the rounds ejected from the gun fly into the air, glance off the bulkhead and disappear down the opening of my tee-shirt. Instantly I felt a searing sensation on my stomach! With a yowl, I jumped up, clawed at my tee-shirt, ripped its tails out of my trousers, and let a red-hot 50-caliber round drop with a clank into the bilge. There at my belt line, burned into the flesh of my stomach was the perfect impression of the 50-caliber brass cartridge! Boy, did that sting!

Fearing that I was marked for life with the silhouette of a 50-caliber round burned into me, I went to the dispensary to obtain some ointment. The corpsman gave me very little pity, knowing that the regulations required full clothing or flight suits to be worn at all times for the crew's protection against burns.

The cartridge-shaped scar eventually disappeared, and I remained unmarked for the rest of the war.

NORFOLK, VIRGINIA

My final flight in operational training was on September 10, 1943, almost a year to the day since I reported in to the pre-flight school at St. Mary's in California. I had become qualified in all of the courses laid down, and was now considered able to fit in with the duties of an operating squadron overseas.

Since I was due for overseas duty, I was given fourteen days leave before reporting to the Commandant, Naval Air Station, Norfolk, Virginia, for further orders.

In making one final look around the house I found the diary I had kept while attending college at Wayne.

I took time to write the following:

"September 18, 1943—I haven't written in my diary for a long time, namely because I haven't been here. I've been in St. Mary's, Norman, Corpus Christi and Jacksonville. I leave for Norfolk,

Virginia, tomorrow at 2:30. I finally got my wings and from now on we aren't fooling. We're going to form a squadron and get our regular crews. We may be there a couple of months or we may shove off right away. At any rate, we're done fooling.

"September 19, 1943—I go in an hour or so. I may not get a chance to write again. So long."

Upon reporting in to Norfolk, Virginia, I was assigned temporary housing at the Transient Officers' Quarters, and I was told to check in every morning at about 0900 to see if my orders had arrived.

As I checked into the Transient Officers' Quarters, I met Ensign Jim Cain and Ensign Jack Snare, my two shipmates from Jacksonville. They too, were awaiting orders. We had a real reunion. We discussed the happy possibility that we all three might be assigned the same squadron, though it seemed highly improbable.

For almost a month the three of us dutifully checked in with the Officer of the Day, seeking our orders. Finding none had arrived, we would go into town and look at the tattoo parlors, and jokingly dared each other to go get tattooed. We never did, however.

Since all three of us were from small midwestern towns, the many burlesque houses were a novelty. We went to one, were unimpressed and never went to another.

Finally we found the base hobby shop, and since both Snare and I had built models when we were younger, we bought some supplies and proceeded to build a model of the Spitfire. It seemed an odd way to prepare for war.

Our orders arrived on October 20, directing us to report to Lt. Robert Beaudine, USN, for transportation to Patrol Squadron 73. We all three were assigned to VP-73.

Lt. Beaudine was located down at the flight line, looking over a brand-new PBY-5A, our transport to the squadron. With him was Lt. Harry Larsen, also of VP-73. Upon reporting to them we were told that VP-73 was currently based at Agadir, French Morocco, and following acceptance of the new ship, we would leave for French Morocco.

For two days, October 26 and 27, we ran acceptance tests on

the new plane. It had a total of ten hours on it, and smelled just like a new car, all clean and lacquery from the paint. There would be seven of us aboard the Catalina Bureau No. 34047, Lts. Beaudine and Larsen, we three Ensigns, the plane captain and the radioman.

After over four hours of testing, Lt. Beaudine, our PPC, was satisfied that all was in order and told us we would leave at 0500 on October 28 for Deland, Florida, our first stop on the way to French Morocco.

Every sailor we talked to expressed his desire to get out of Norfolk, Virginia. We were no different. We'd had enough of loafing.

SPIRIT OF ST. VITIS II

Navy air crews envied their counterparts in the Army Air Corps for the nose art adorning their war planes. Not only was such personal decoration frowned upon by the Navy brass, but in Navy aerial operations it would have been impractical, since Navy air crews were not assigned one plane for their exclusive use. In our squadron, for example, it was rare that we flew the same PBY twice in a row. We could be assigned any one of twelve planes attached. The crew members remained constant, but not the aircraft.

On the evening of October 27, all testing and loading of our PBY having been completed, we stood beside it admiring its pristine paint job and immaculate condition.

"You know what?" I said. "We ought to name it like the Army does."

"That's a good idea," said Ensign Cain. "What'll we call it?"

We asked all of the crew if they had any suggestions, and they had none, except they were all definite in the opinion the plane should have a name.

Inasmuch as no one came forth with an appropriate name, I spoke up and suggested we call it *Spirit of St. Vitis II.*

It was agreeable to all to give the plane that name, but one of them asked why I picked that name.

I told them this story:

I was six and a half years old when Lindbergh made the first solo crossing of the Atlantic in the Ryan monoplane, *Spirit of St. Louis*. My ambition was to fly the Atlantic and do it in a Spirit of St. Louis.

In 1928 two friends and I built a push-mobile airplane big enough for us to get into. It was made of lath and covered with my brother Orv's pup tent. Wooden wagon wheels enabled it to roll roughly over the ground as we pushed it along.

Since none of us was able to print, let alone spell, we asked my older brother, Frank, if he would paint *Spirit of St. Louis* on the nose. Of course he agreed.

As he squatted beside the plane, paint brush in hand, he said, "You know, the way this thing shimmies and shakes when you push it, you ought to call it *Spirit of St. Vitis.*"

That was okay with us, and as a result, that is the name our plane was given.

For over a year we "flew" in our plane, and finally, as we either outgrew it or got tired of it, we burned it. But, I went on to explain, I never forgot our trusty airplane. It was a fighter, bomber, two- and three-motored one, a stunt plane and an ocean-crosser. It could do anything.

Upon hearing this story, the crew members became more enthusiastic about the name, and one asked, "Okay, now how do we get the name put on?"

Noting that it was still early in the evening, I replied, "Ship's Service will be open; I'll go and get some black shoe polish with a dauber, and use that for paint."

Obtaining a bottle of black Shinola liquid shoe polish, I printed on both sides of the bow of our new P-boat the legend, *Spirit of St. Vitis II.*

During the early morning hours of October 28, 1943, we took off from the runway of Norfolk, Virginia, bound for Agadir,

French Morocco. Our first stop would be Deland, Florida, where we would be briefed on the Air Transport Command's route to Africa via South America and the South Atlantic.

My lifelong ambition was soon to be realized. I had learned to fly as Lindbergh had, I was about to fly the Atlantic—albeit the South Atlantic, not the North as Lindy had—and I was doing it not in the *Spirit of St. Louis,* but in a PBY-5A, the *Spirit of St. Vitis II.*

DELAND

When the Air Transport Command was formed early in the war, one of its primary routes for ferrying planes to the battlefronts was via South America, across the South Atlantic to Liberia in Africa and on across the dark continent to Egypt, the Middle East, or on to India and China. All aircraft being flown to eastern destinations used this well-established route, and were under the jurisdiction of the ATC.

Six hours after our take-off from Norfolk we were landing at the ATC base in Deland, Florida.

Upon checking into Operations, we were advised that there would be a briefing at 1400 for all aircraft now en route overseas, and all crews were instructed to attend. Three Martin Baltimore crews, en route to Egypt with planes for the Royal Australian Air Force, joined us at the briefing. At the briefing, Air Corps experts went over the fine points of surviving in the event of a forced landing in the South American jungle, pointing out such appetizing items as which lizards and snakes were edible and how to find the most nourishing bugs and plants. Further lectures included how to ditch at sea, which was familiar to the Navy crew, and emergency communications.

One of the most interesting lectures given was the one about the approaches to the many airfields en route to Africa. Slides were shown of the various air bases illustrating how they appeared to an airplane approaching from many different altitudes and directions. By the time we finished we knew exactly what the airfield looked like and where any obstructions might be located. That, we thought, was worth seeing, as many foreign airports did not have our same obstruction symbols.

The ground crews at the ATC base at Deland were very helpful and cooperative. They went out of their way to see that the refueling was done promptly, and that any supplies needed were procured for us immediately.

The briefings and final preparations for the over-water flight to San Juan, Puerto Rico, were finished at 1730, and Jim and Jack and I decided to go for a walk around the base in order to stretch our legs. As we strolled along one side of the base, we found a canal bordering the field, and decided to follow it. As we walked, we were aware of a disturbance in the water, and suddenly an enormous head, almost human, came up out of the dark waters of the canal. The beady eyes peered at us, then it slowly sank into the murky water as a spoonlike tail slapped the water.

We were horrified, and stood transfixed until we heard a man chuckle behind us. "That, boys, is a manatee. He looks fierce, but he is harmless and eats only seaweed and grasses on the canal bottoms." He went on to explain that the early sailors thought manatees were human-fish, and the stories of mermaids came from sightings of the huge animal.

Thanking the stranger for this bit of wisdom, all three of us resolved never to go even wading in a Florida canal . . . the manatees might forget they are supposed to be harmless.

As darkness came over Deland, we sought out the Transient Officers' Barracks and hit the sack. Tomorrow, the 29th, we'd be flying all day to San Juan, Puerto Rico, our first stop away from the United States.

RUM-RUNNER

The ten-hour flight from Deland to San Juan, Puerto Rico, was uneventful, although it was over the most beautiful blue water any of us had seen. Our course skirted Cuba by many miles, and though we flew over numerous cays, our nearest approach to land on the long flight was the Dominican Republic, and that was far off to starboard, over the horizon.

Late in the afternoon we touched down at NAS, San Juan, and after securing the *Spirit of St. Vitis II* and turning the refueling chores over to the ground crew, we set off for the Transient Quarters for the night.

As the station carry-all drove us past the Officers' Club, both Lt. Beaudine and Lt. Larsen seemed to come alive. Lt. Larsen fumbled in the pockets of his flight suit and came up with what appeared to be a list of names, as on an order blank. He explained to us three Ensigns that when they left the squadron at Agadir to come to Norfolk to pick up the new plane and ferry us back, many of the squadron mates had asked them to bring back various and sundry items of liquor. So that no order would be missed, this list had been made.

Our driver agreed to stop at the "O" Club, and we piled out of the carry-all and in a few moments were standing before the bartender with the liquor orders.

I never was much of a drinker, and as a result, this stock of whiskey, wine, gin, vodka and rum overwhelmed me. Mostly the rum. Boy, how they ordered rum. Looking back, the popularity of rum probably stemmed from the widely sung tune of the day, "Drinking Rum and Coca-Cola," and from the highball Cuba Libre, a less costly potable than many of the others.

With the help of the barkeep, our driver and the rest of us loaded the packaged bottles into the carry-all, and instead of going directly to the Transient Officers' Barracks, we detoured around back to the flight line and, seeing it deserted, loaded our contraband into the PBY. Due to the extra weight of the bottled goods, we ran another weight and balance on the loading to be certain we were not going to be tail-heavy when we took off in the morning. This took almost two hours to accomplish due to the shifting and reshifting of the equipment (and liquor) needed to distribute the load properly. By 2000 the task was completed, and we finally arrived at the barracks and hit the sack.

At dawn we were at the flight line with all of our gear, ready for the next leg to Georgetown, British Guiana. Once loaded, we taxied out for take-off.

Ensign Cain was flying co-pilot for Lt. Beaudine. Lt. Larsen and Ensign Snare were in the afterstation, and I was in the nav comparment directly behind the cockpit with the radioman.

With the advancing of the throttles, the PBY began rolling down the runway. As the ship accelerated to take-off speed, I could see and feel the nose rise steeply. Both Lt. Beaudine and Ensign Cain were exerting all of their strength pushing the yoke forward. Lt. Beaudine was frantically cranking the elevator trim tab to the "nose down" position. We were out of trim, and about to stall!

Ensign Cain, who had one hand free, put his microphone to his lips and called on the intercom for everyone in the afterstation to come forward immediately. Ensign Snare and Lt. Larsen scrambled over the liquor cases and assorted gear and dove headfirst into the nav comparment. With the weight aft removed, the plane became docile. Once trim was restored, we repositioned the baggage, some even up in the nose compartment, and experienced no further trouble. But had Ensign Cain not called for Lt. Larsen and Ensign Snare to come forward, the news headlines might have read, "PBY LOADED WITH RUM CRASHES IN PUERTO RICO."

TO NATAL

More than ten hours after our dicey take-off at San Juan we landed at Atkinson Field in Georgetown, British Guiana. Here, on the edge of the vast rain forest, we got our first look at the South American jungle. We had no desire to venture off the base; rather, we went to the mosquito-net-lined Operations tent and visited with the pilots of the Martin Baltimore crews we had met in Deland. They too, had contraband from San Juan.

Dawn on October 31 saw us in the air once more, bound for Belém, Brazil. Rather than fly the more circuitous route along the coast, we elected to fly direct, over the trackless jungles of the

Amazon. At no time during the eight-hour flight did we see any sign of civilization, only the deep green of the rain forests below. Occasionally a wisp of smoke would be seen rising from the black green below, providing a clue of some life in the jungle.

The delta of the Amazon was an awe-inspiring sight. It is hundreds of miles across, and it seemed to take forever for us to cross it in the *Spirit of St. Vitis II*. Hundreds of islets and streams laced the area, all deeply enshrouded in dark-green foliage. Far out to sea, extending for one hundred miles, fanned the dirty, clay-colored water of the Amazon, making a sharp contrast with the deep blue of the ocean. According to the ATC personnel at Atkinson Field, the Amazon discharges more water into the Atlantic than the world's next three largest rivers combined, and freshens the Atlantic waters over one hundred miles offshore.

As we crossed the equator at 49° 24" W, we had an impromptu ceremony of toasting each other with paper cups filled with tepid water. Had we been on a ship at sea the ceremonies would have been more hilarious, with King Neptune, Shellbacks, Polliwogs and their many assistants.

Belém, located on the delta of the Tocantins River, was an eight-hour flight from Atkinson Field at Georgetown, British Guiana. It was in this area that one-time football great Tom Harmon, a Lieutenant in the Army Air Corps, bailed out of his crippled bomber and spent several days in the steaming jungle before he was rescued by friendly Indians and Brazilian soldiers. He was lucky, as hostile natives swarmed in the teeming rain forests.

The town of Belém was within walking distance of the Air Transport facility, and since it was close by, we walked into town after landing and securing the PBY. The Air Corps people had warned us against drinking the water or eating any of the food we might want to sample.

The dirty, dusty street, the dilapidated, crumbling stucco buildings and the grimy, poorly dressed natives caused us to turn back and head for the safety and orderliness of the airfield.

As we trudged back to the base, a youthful Brazilian boy followed a few feet behind us yelling, "Hey, Yanquis, Zig Zig my sister. Real cheap!" He was some enterprising entrepreneur, but we were not interested. Another flight of over eight hours brought us to the jumping-off place for the South Atlantic crossing, Natal. By far the most modern airfield we had encountered thus far, it reminded us of an air base back in the States.

During each leg of the flight so far we had run stringent fuel consumption tests. We discovered that the flight to Ascension Island, located in mid-Atlantic, could well tax the extreme range of the *Spirit of St. Vitis II*. Loaded as we were with the necessities ordered by the squadron mates in Agadir, it was doubtful whether we could make it to the island. So we decided to fly to the Navy repair facility at Receife, where we would have the leak-proof and bullet-proof bladders removed from the gas tank to give us more fuel capacity.

It was there I met Spike.

SPIKE

An hour-and-a-half flight from Natal to Receife gave us plenty of time to tour the city once the plane was in the hands of the maintenance people at the Naval Air Facility.

A mixture of new and old Portugal, Receife swarmed with itinerant merchants from the jungle communities hawking their wares. As we walked down a cobblestone street, we came upon a vendor specializing in the sale of a spider monkey. The monkey was irresistible. He was about eight inches tall, with a head the size of a golf ball. He had jug-handle ears and an honest face. All covered with silky brown fur, he was not one to forget easily.

I had never owned a pet as a kid, but I was determined to have one now. Lacking any Brazilian money, I bartered with the owner and finally closed the transaction by offering a package of Lucky Strike cigarettes and a pocket comb in exchange for the little fellow. I named him Spike.

In no time at all, Spike had us all wrapped around his tiny fingers. The cord leash around his neck wasn't necessary, as Spike was sublimely happy with the members of his Navy family. He would roam from one of our shoulders to another, climbing over our heads, using our ears for toeholds and chattering all the while. Spike stayed with me in the Transient Quarters, and spent the night curled up on my shaving kit, dreaming whatever spider monkeys dream.

The next day our PBY was ready and we flew back to Natal to refuel for the long hop to Ascension. We planned on leaving at 2100 in order to make a daylight approach to the tiny mid-Atlantic island.

Lts. Beaudine and Larsen were in the cockpit; Spike and I, along with the radioman, were in the navigation compartment, and Ensigns Cain and Snare were in the afterstation blisters (we had reloaded everything after the San Juan fiasco).

Promptly at 2100 the wheels of our PBY began to roll, and in a few minutes we were off the ground, and the lights of Natal were dropping away rapidly.

Since I was doing the navigating on this first portion of the leg, I told the radioman to tune in on the Natal radio range, and with another of his radios to dial in the Ascension beam. Both ranges met in mid-ocean. All Lt. Beaudine had to do was fly the beam out toward the island. I took a few celestial shots to determine our ground speed, and all went well. Actually, the navigation was easy as long as the radios worked, which they did.

At dawn Ensign Cain relieved me at the navigator's table, and I got into the left seat while Lt. Beaudine sacked out in the bunks.

Spike was cuddled down in the inside pocket of my flight jacket, sound asleep. Around noon, his nap over, Spike stuck his head out of my pocket and emerged, ready to face his new world. Tying one end of the cord to the control column, I let Spike have the run of the cockpit. Due to the heat we had all of the windows and vents open, but this didn't bother Spike a bit. Lt. Larsen and I had a chart spread out between us, and Spike, noticing the throttles and prop controls on the overhead, leaped up and grabbed them, swinging from them as though they were tree branches, chattering merrily all the while.

Suddenly, without warning, Spike forgot his manners. As he

swung, he let everything go! To this day I wonder how that little thing could hold so much. Diffused by the wind from the open windows, a mist was produced that rendered visibility in the cockpit zero-zero. It covered everything, dissolving even the printing on the chart. When our eyes stopped smarting, Spike was reeled in and put in a box supplied by the plane captain. His showing off had spread through the plane. Spike continued the trip in the box, and upon landing at Ascension, Spike and I were the first off. The first person to meet us was an Army sergeant, and I made him a present of Spike. We didn't tell him of Spike's misconduct.

LONELY ASCENSION ISLAND

The thirteen-and-a-half-hour flight from Natal to Ascension was mostly uneventful, with the exception of little Spike's misdeed.

On the thirty-four-square-mile island of volcanic rock and ash, there was only one scraggly tree, struggling for survival in the base Commander's compound. I doubt whether Spike will ever get to use it.

While the Air Corps personnel refueled our PBY, the rest of us, under the direction of the plane captain, checked the ship for the next overwater leg to Roberts Field in Liberia. Having finished that, and with the *Spirit of St. Vitis II* secured, we were taken to our quarters.

En route to the barracks, our driver asked us if we'd like to take a tour of the island and hunt for some octopuses. We thought that was a good idea, and after cooling off, we met our host and set off for the beach—but not before I had hunted through my gear for the knife my brother Orv had made for me. It was fashioned from a World War I bayonet and had a blade almost a foot long. I took this instead of my Navy-issue sheath knife, whose blade was much shorter. I wanted to stay as far away as I could from any octopus I might find.

The sand on Ascension's beaches was a yellow color, resembling very coarse corn meal, and seemed to have no rough edges. The rocks were black volcanic projections, and covered the island. When United States forces built the airfield, thousands of tons of TNT had to be used to level the runway areas.

Our Army driver took us to the edge of the water and pointed out the many tidal pools left when the water receded. By looking very closely and probing with our knives, we could feel the squishy bodies of the octopus, so concealed by his protective coloring he was nearly invisible. Once disturbed, he would dart to the other side of the pool, discharging a black inky substance as he shot away, and flatten himself almost hidden against the rocks. I was glad I had a long knife blade.

Our guide had brought a couple of glass jars, and when we had captured two of the eight-armed creatures he put them and some sea water in the jars, and generously offered them to us as pets. We graciously refused his offer, and that evening as we turned in, we went by his quarters in the barracks, and saw the two jars sitting proudly on his bookshelf.

I, for one, didn't feel too badly about turning down his offer. I had had enough trouble with Spike.

We were glad to leave Ascension; it must have been the most forgotten outpost in the Atlantic, and the servicemen there certainly must have struggled to maintain their sanity, as lonely as it was. At first light on November 6 we took off for Roberts Field. Though we crossed the equator again, we had no ceremonies this time. Crossing equators was getting to be old hat—certainly nothing to get excited about. Eight hours and twenty minutes after leaving Ascension we were circling the Air Transport Command Base at Roberts Field in Liberia, located in the center of a vast rubber plantation owned by the Firestone Rubber Company.

Upon landing we felt suffocated by the humidity and extreme heat of Africa. The Air Corps people, who were used to the temperature, took pity on us. They explained that they were given a ration of one can of beer a day at the Enlisted Men's Club, and they would give us each a can if we liked. We liked. As I have mentioned earlier, I was not much of a drinker, but that was one time I appreciated a can of beer. It was the best thing I ever drank!

Our quarters on the plantation were first rate, and as I went to sleep I wondered how Spike was getting along back there on Ascension Island.

SHORT-SNORTER

It was over an eight-hour flight from Roberts Field to Port Étienne, Mauritania. Using radar to maintain our distance from the coast we paralleled the shores of North Africa headed for Agadir, French Morocco. We made it very clear to the officials at Dakar that we were well beyond the three-mile limit. There were many Vichy French there, and they were not too friendly to Americans. We would give them no excuse to become upset by our passage up the coast. Port Étienne was the base of a Royal Air Force Sunderland squadron, with the Atlantic Ocean on one side and the Sahara on the other. The Sunderlands were our counterparts in the British forces, performing anti-submarine patrols, convoy coverage and air rescue missions, as we did.

Our PBY was almost dwarfed by the huge Sunderlands, both in size and weight. Because of their many power turrets and machine gun positions, the Luftwaffe had labeled them "Porcupines." They were not amphibious, as was our PBY; they were strictly flying boats.

The RAF crews were very cordial to us and insisted we sample their warm British beer and eat a lunch of boiled potatoes and tripe. After lunch the pilots showed us around their base and gave us a first-hand look at their aircraft. One of them, Flight Officer Jack Strain, lamented that he hadn't had any chocolate since arriving in Africa several months ago, and he was almost beside himself when I gave him a partial box of Hershey's. In return, he gave me an RAF emergency packet to be used in case of forced landings, and a little book on the adventures of Pilot Officer P.O. Prune, the RAF's version of Dilbert Dunker, the fictional boob who does nothing right.

It was F.O. Strain who introduced us to and inducted us into the "Short Snorters" Club. Pilot Strain explained that when Prime Minister Winston Churchill was returning from his first flying visit with President Roosevelt aboard an Air Corps B-24, he asked all of the crew members to put their signatures on a piece of paper money along with his. He then had each of them produce a paper bill, and each one signed each of the others. All of them were instructed to write on the edge of the bill their name, preceded by the caption, "Short-Snorter." The time and place of the signing was also inscribed on the money. "You are now Short-Snorters," he said, "and anytime you hear anyone boast of flying the Atlantic, ask them to produce their Short-Snorter bill. If they have one, and produce it, so be it. If it is not produced, they stand drinks for all in the pub."

My Short-Snorter is dated November 7, 1943, at Port Étienne, Mauritania.

That night, before turning in, Ensign Cain and I walked to the edge of the base and climbed to the top of a giant sand dune that encroached on the land by the sea. As we struggled through the ankle-deep sand we met an Arab standing there in the half-light, looking for all the world like a character from *Beau Geste*. Though he was no doubt friendly, we took no chances and went back to the base as fast as we could wade through the sand.

The flight from Port Étienne to the Naval Air Facility, Ben Sergao Field, Agadir, French Morocco, was the shortest one of the whole trip. After six hours of following the coast and cautiously staying clear of Spain's Canary Islands, we sighted the Portuguese fort overlooking Agadir, and, in the fading light, the former Air France airport, now used by the United States Navy's Patrol Squadron 73.

PATROL SQUADRON 73

During our flight from Norfolk, Virginia to Agadir, both Lts. Beaudine and Larsen told us some of the background of the unit.

The squadron was originally commissioned on September 1,

1936 as Patrol Squadron 15 (VP-15) at Annapolis, Maryland. On July 1, 1939, while under the command of Lt. Cdr. A.P. Storrs, USN, the squadron designation was changed to Patrol Squadron 53 (VP-53). After duties in the Caribbean, the squadron returned to San Diego for new planes, then went to Norfolk, Virginia to be transferred to Quonset Point, Rhode Island.

On July 1, 1941, Lt. Cdr. James Edward Leeper, USN, was promoted from Executive Officer to Commanding Officer, and the designation was again changed to Patrol Squadron 73 (VP-73).

During the Neutrality Patrol of the U.S.A., the squadron was assigned to the command of Patrol Wing 7, Task Force 24, of the U.S. Atlantic Fleet.

In early August 1942, Lt. Cdr. Leeper was relieved as Commanding Officer of Patrol Squadron 73 by Lt. Cdr. Alexander S. Heyward.

On August 10, 1942, the first division of the squadron was stationed at Fleet Air Base, Reykjavik, Iceland; the second division was stationed at USNAS Argentia, Newfoundland. In that same month Lt. Gerald Duffy sighted the first German U-boat and reported it.

On August 20, 1942, while escorting a British task force, 73-P-9 sighted a U-boat on the surface. The Patrol Plane Commander (PPC), Lt. (jg.) Robert B. Hopgood, dove to attack while the U-boat fired on his plane, dropping his bombs in a perfect straddle on the U-boat. The center bomb dropped directly on the sub and stuck in the wooden grating on the deck. The other bombs exploded in the water, but apparently did no very serious damage. On the other hand, the one that landed on deck inflicted fatal damage when it was pushed over the side by a member of the sub's crew. As soon as it reached its set depth to explode, it did so. Hopgood sent a message to the base, "Sank sub, open club." (This referred to the edict by the Commander of the air base at Iceland, the task force Commander, that the Officers' Club would be closed until the squadron got a U-boat.) The British recovered fifty-two prisoners from the U-boat, which turned out to be a re-supply sub.

In the first week of November, 1942, the squadron departed Iceland for eventual assignment to Morocco. On November 12, the day after the invasion of North Africa, the squadron deployed to its assigned base, the French Naval Air Station, Port Lyautey, French Morocco. ASW patrols were started immediately, covering all seaward approaches to the Moroccan coast.

A few months later VP-73 moved down the coast to a small airport at Agadir, French Morocco. Conditions were much more primitive than at Port Lyautey; all hands lived in tents, and the flies were plentiful.

On September 5, 1943, Lt. Cdr. John Odell, Jr., the squadron's Executive Officer, relieved Lt. Cdr. Heyward as Commanding Officer.

On October 1, 1943, 73-P-3 developed engine trouble on takeoff and crashed three miles south of Ben Sergao Field (the official name of the Agadir airport). Lt. (jg.) Robert J. Fuchs and his entire crew of eight were lost.

On October 10, 1943, 73-P-10 was attacked by a Spanish Fiat CR-42 in the vicinity of Gran Canaris Island. Gunfire was exchanged, with some damage to the aircraft.

On November 1, 1943, 73-P-11 was attacked by a CR-42 near Melenara Point, Gran Canaris Island. The Fiat, apparently damaged by the PBY's port blister gunner, glided toward land. Plane 11 was extensively damaged, and three men aboard were wounded.

That brought us pretty well up to date.

LOVE

Ensign Dan Perch was of the opinion that he was no longer "lucky in love." Here he was in French Morocco with Patrol Squadron 73, while his fiancee, Lt. Elsie Getz, Army Nurse Corps, was stationed with the 105th Station Hospital near Bizerte, Tunisia, some twelve hundred miles northeast across the Sahara and the Atlas Mountains, somewhere on the shores of the Mediterranean Sea. Though Ensign Perch knew the location of Lt. Getz, she had no idea where he was. Dan sought to remedy that situation as soon as possible.

REACHING THE GOAL

Shortly after Lt. Cdr. John Odell, Jr. assumed command of the squadron on September 5, 1943, a quaking Ensign Perch approached him. It was the first time either had met.

Dan presented his case to the skipper. Could he be granted time off in order to visit his fiancee in Bizerte? Cdr. Odell listened patiently as the young Ensign talked.

"How long have you known the young lady?" he asked. "Since 1938, Sir," replied Ensign Perch. "We met on a blind date in Toledo when she was in nurses' training. In 1943, after she enlisted in the Army Nurse Corps, she was sent overseas with the 105th Station Hospital somewhere near Bizerte. That same year I was commissioned at Corpus Christi and sent to VP-73. She doesn't know I'm over here in Africa."

Assured that Ensign Perch was not engaged in a fly-by-night romance, the skipper thought for a moment, then said, "You have just reported to the squadron, and won't be flying for ten days. You might as well go see your young lady." He was given a VIP priority pass on MATS aircraft.

Tossing a snappy salute, Ensign Perch turned and almost ran to his Quonset. Though he planned on wearing his khaki uniform, his tentmates, Al Laliberti and Joe Loper, insisted he wear his Navy aviation greens. They even made him take off his high-top suede marine combat boondockers and put on his brown dress oxfords. "If you're going to see your fiancee, you want to be dressed up neatly," they advised him. Then, grabbing his green cloth Navy suitcase, he hurried to the flight line, where a Military Air Transport R4D flew him to Bizerte. He had no papers, and could have been considered AWOL; fortunately he was not challenged at any time during this adventure.

It had rained heavily in Bizerte, and Ensign Perch climbed out of the R4D to step into ankle-deep mud. He wished Laliberte and Loper would have let him wear his high boondockers. He immediately tried to find the U.S. Army Headquarters, and was informed that it was five miles north of the airport.

Hitchhiking up the muddy road was easy, as it teemed with military vehicles. Upon reaching Army Headquarters, Ensign Perch asked the location of the 105th Station Hospital. A search of the files revealed that the 105th didn't have any nurses; they had all been transferred to other hospitals! Some of the staff thought she had been reassigned to a unit north on some Italian island. A further search of the files located her. "She's with the 33rd General Hospital, across from the airfield where you landed," announced one of the clerks happily.

A very elated VP-73 pilot joyously hitchhiked over the muddy, bombed-out road back to the Bizerte airport. Locating a field telephone, he attempted to call her. At best, the connections on any field telephone are poor, and this one was typical. In order to be heard, Dan felt obliged to yell into the mouthpiece, and Lt. Getz did the same. Everyone in the hangar and in the hospital were aware of the reunion. That evening, with Elsie off duty, they had a joyful reunion, standing with the mud oozing over their shoe tops.

A month later Ensign Perch officially returned to Bizerte and started the paperwork necessary for him to marry Lt. Getz. Six months and forty-four forms later, permission was granted. Even General Eisenhower's office was involved. Before the wedding bells tolled, Lt. Getz was sent to Anzio, and Ensign Perch was reassigned to New York. In January 1945, they were married in New York.

AGADIR, FRENCH MOROCCO

In both 1905 and 1911, the seacoast town of Agadir, French Morocco, was in the world news. Caused by a confrontation of the French and Germans, the "Moroccan Crises" ended with the Germans withdrawing their warships from the Moroccan port. Agadir had become well known.

A stop-over of the great French flier and writer Antoine de Sainte-Exupery, Agadir was one of the principal airmail fields of the Latecoere Line, which was the pioneer in trans-Atlantic airmail service to South America in the 1920s. The line became Air France in 1932.

REACHING THE GOAL

In 1943 the runways were of crushed rock and clay. The original hangars were still in use by Air France, and prehistoric Amiot 143s built in 1934 regularly landed to disembark and load their passengers. The Amiots had been inherited from the Armée de L'Air following the fall of France.

Pyramid tents, each housing four men, made up the living quarters of the squadron. Graveled walks connected all parts of the camp. The Officers' Club and the Enlisted Men's Club were tents also, the O Club located at one end of a "street," the EM Club situated at the other.

Operations, too, was housed in a tent, larger than the rest, and contained the radio facilities, the briefing office and the Air Combat Intelligence Officer.

It was nearly dark when we landed, and by the time we had logged in with the Duty Officer and carried our gear to our assigned tent, the night was pitch black.

It took some time to get our gear properly stowed and our sleeping bags unpacked and put on our cots—all of this done in lantern-light.

The Duty Officer had given us directions to the head, and I was the last one to require its use. My tent-mates, Ensign Snare and Ensign Cain, were fast asleep when I finished getting located and needed to use the head.

I had just started down the stony path when I spotted a campfire nearby with a cluster of Arabs squatting about it. Having heard stories of the alleged treatment the Arabs gave lone servicemen at Port Étienne, I went back to my tent and strapped on my loaded Colt .45. I then returned to the head and sat there with the .45 in my hand, ready to sell my life dearly if those Arabs tried anything.

All of this time I could hear the mumbled chatter of the tribesmen gathered about the fire.

In a short time I returned to my tent with my .45 safely holstered, and crawled into my sleeping bag.

I was awakened in the morning by the bustle of activity, not only within our tent, but from the outside as well. I pulled on a pair of trousers and looked out the tent-flap. The area was alive with my squadron mates, all anxious to meet the new day.

I was curious about the Arabs. Where had they gone?

As I walked toward the head, I noticed a sturdy wire mesh fence encircling the airfield. Barbed wire graced its top, making it nearly unassailable. Sentries paced its perimeter. Some one hundred feet on the other side of the fence crouched a group of burnoose-clad followers of Allah, gesturing and talking near the smoldering embers of a campfire. In the dark of night I hadn't been able to see the fence. I didn't have to worry; those fellows couldn't have gotten to me if they had tried.

GIBRALTAR

Without a doubt, the most boring duty in the squadron was serving on the Alert Crew. This twenty-four-hour assignment consisted of standing by the fully armed PBY with the entire crew at hand, ready to be airborne within fifteen minutes of notification by Operations or the Duty Officer.

The Alert Crew could be dispatched as the result of a U-boat sighting, a sinking, or any kind of emergency—even when some VIP fancied he needed immediate air transportation in order to complete a vital mission.

My crew and I were scheduled for this duty, and were ready for any emergency that might arise. Some were playing ball under the wing, some were writing letters in the shade the PBY provided, others were napping in the blisters, curled around the 50-caliber gun mounts. My fellow pilots, Lt. Vyrl Leichliter and Ensign Tom Cain, and I were in the Quonset ready room playing acey-deucy. We were anxious for time to pass so that we could secure and pursue more interesting activities in Port Lyautey.

Suddenly the field telephone on the operations desk jangled. The Duty Officer, Lt. (jg.) Graham Dripps, snatched the handset from its cradle and put it to his ear. With a pencil in one hand, he jotted down some notes. With a curt, "We will be ready at once, Sir," he replaced the phone and gave us our mission.

Commandante Paul leConde of the Free French Armée de L'Air was needed at Gibraltar on important business, and we were to fly him there. Furthermore, he was to be transported there now.

All three of us dashed from the hut and jogged to 73-P-10, parked on the perforated metal hard stand by Operations. The crew, seeing us hurrying toward the PBY, went immediately to their pre-flight duties, and by the time we had boarded the plane, the plane captain had the Pratt & Whitneys primed and ready to start.

As Lick and I started the starboard engine, a French Renault staff car pulled up to the after-station ladder and a dapper French officer climbed aboard. He was dressed as though he commanded Fort Zinderneuf.

In twelve minutes our wheels had left the ground. That, we thought, should make Operations happy. We set a course out to sea, then north up the coast to Gibraltar. Carefully we observed the three-mile limit as we paralleled the coast of Spanish Morocco; yet as we approached Tangier we could see the black puffs of flak bursts, evidently fired vertically into the sky so that we would be aware that our presence was known by the Spaniards.

As we neared the Rock, we turned on our IFF to inform the British we were friendly. We were flying at 800 feet, and the monolith of Gibraltar loomed some 500 feet over us. The side facing the strait was almost completely covered with troughed cement, at places reinforced by huge anchor chains, holding the face of the Rock in place. It certainly didn't look like the Prudential Insurance Company advertisements. The troughs, we found out later, were to collect rainwater in the event of a siege.

When we had landed at the Gibraltar airstrip, our passenger hurriedly clambered down the after-station ladder and sped off in another staff car. We decided to tour the Rock.

As our driver careened through the crowded streets of Gibraltar, we noticed a complete lack of car horns blowing. Instead, the drivers beat on the sides of the cars to alert a driver ahead. The listening apparatus used in air raid warnings forbade blowing of horns, we were told.

We strolled through the vast tunnels honeycombing the

fortress, climbed the graveled paths to the top of the Rock and marveled at the miles of stone fences with jagged sheets of broken plate glass embedded in them to thwart enemy parachutists. Huge gun emplacements were spotted at strategic positions overlooking the strait. We also came upon a tribe of Barbary apes clambering over the rocks, and we all agreed they looked and acted like some humans we knew.

THE FIATS

Across the field from VP-73 was a French photo reconnaissance squadron. They flew Vultee A-31 Vengeance dive bombers. This Free French unit worked very closely with us in our battle with the German U-boats.

Off the coast of French Morocco, and very close to Agadir, were the Spanish Canary Islands. Spain, though officially neutral during World War II, strongly supported the Axis in many ways. German submarines would slip out of the ports of Occupied France on the Bay of Biscay, and, before setting out for the shipping lanes in the Atlantic, stop at the Canary port of Las Palmas on Gran Canaris to resupply and charge their batteries.

The Free French photo squadron would fly over the port, taking pictures of the ships tied up at the piers. Being close neighbors of the French, the Spanish did not seem to be upset by the constant surveillance missions flown by the Vultees.

The photographs of the Canary Island port were turned over to our Air Combat Intelligence (ACI) men. If, in their opinion, a vessel resembling either a surface raider or a U-boat appeared in the photos, we flew a barrier patrol outside the harbor's mouth, in international waters, until the ship emerged for either identification or possible attack.

On October 10, while Ensigns Cain, Snare and I had been languishing in Norfolk, Virginia, one of VP-73's PBYs was attacked by a Spanish Fiat CR-42 and sustained some damage from the

Spanish machine-gun fire. The PBY finally eluded the Fiat by flying into some providential clouds nearby, and escaped.

On November 1 another battle between VP-73 and a Spanish Fiat took place over the Canaries. The PBY flown by Lt. William Hoffman, Patrol Plane Commander (PPC) and co-pilots Lt. (jg.) E.T.J. "Gabby" Hartnett, and Lt. (jg.) W.H. Abram was attacked without warning by a Spanish fighter which had been concealed in the clouds.

On the first firing pass, the Spanish Fiat succeeded in knocking out Lt. Hoffman's starboard engine and puncturing the starboard gas tank, in addition to wounding ACMM E.D. White, ACMM3c V.A. Pavao, ACMM3c R.G. Hudson and ARMIc W.J. Pawlek. Lt. Hoffman put the PBY into a steep dive to pick up speed, and at the same time he fishtailed from side to side to give his waist gunners an opportunity to fire on the Fiat. The gunners saw their tracers go home, but the Spaniard returned for two more attacks. Aided by co-pilots Hartnett and Abram, the propeller on the crippled engine was feathered, and evasive tactics were flown in an effort to elude the fighter. More than forty hits were recorded on the Catalina, but at the end of the third attack the fighter fell off and dropped toward the sea.

The PBY crew took stock. One engine was gone. The radios were damaged beyond repair. The landing gear was shot to pieces. Four men were wounded, and a three-hundred-mile trip to a friendly base lay ahead. Below was enemy water.

The P-boat headed home. The bombs were jettisoned, and all removable equipment was dumped over the side to lighten the ship. Hours later, a few miles from the base, the PBY made a crash landing in the bay at Agadir. She was so full of holes she wouldn't float, but a sub-chaser was standing by to pick up the crew.

On April 22, 1944, the crew of 73-P-11 was decorated with the Air Medal, and those wounded were awarded the Purple Heart. The long delay in acknowledging their heroism stemmed from the fact that the original citation read, "In aerial combat with an enemy fighter." Spain was not an enemy; she was neutral. The final citation read, "In combat with a hostile fighter." That the Fiat was "hostile" was certainly putting it mildly.

AIRCRAFT IDENTIFICATION

Following the air battle between our PBY and the Spanish Fiat, the Moroccan Sea Frontier became a beehive of activity. Even before the P-boat was salvaged from the bay at Agadir, a squadron of Navy Vega Ventura PV-1s was called down from Oran.

The squadron's mission was simple: to fly over the Canaries at minimum altitude to entice the Spanish Fiats to engage them in combat. Should the Spaniards elect to intercept the Venturas, they would find they were dealing with a much more dangerous foe than they had encountered in our PBY Catalinas. The PVs carried two fixed forward-firing 50-caliber machine guns in the nose, two 50-caliber guns in the dorsal power turret, and two .303 guns in the rear-firing ventral position. They had a maximum speed of over 300 mph, and they could deal handily with any threat that might arise from the Spanish fighters in the Canaries.

All flights by the French recon squadron were suspended, as were all flights of VP-73 on barrier patrols of the port of Las Palmas, until the PVs had finished their mission.

No Spanish fighters rose to challenge the American Venturas.

While the Canaries were being buzzed by the PVs, our ordinance men obtained a supply of Thompson sub-machine guns and were giving all of the squadron instruction in their use. The Tommy guns would add to the firepower of the two free 50-caliber guns in the waist, our main armament.

And, as if that were not enough activity, we three new Ensigns, Cain, Snare and I, were being indoctrinated with the squadron policies and training syllabus.

On November 18 Lt. Vryl Leichliter became the PPC of my first operational flight. Lt. (jg.) Burton Hovde was PPIP (co-pilot) and I, being the newest member of the crew, was the PP2P (second pilot).

At this stage of the war the Navy patrol squadrons did not have a specialized crew member to serve as navigator, so all pilots were trained in all phases of navigation: dead-reckoning, radio, radar and celestial. It was squadron policy that the newest member of the squadron, as part of his indoctrination, would navigate to the convoy, i.e., out. While flying the coverage patterns around the vessels, the PPIP (co-pilot) would plot the positions and would, when the time came to depart from the ships, do the navigating back to the base. It was always easier to navigate home, for it was very difficult to miss the entire continent of Africa!

Even though we were not on a barrier patrol of the Canary harbors on this flight, each of us had been issued a Tommy gun in the event the Fiats should reappear and because our homeward course would bring us in close proximity to the Spanish islands.

Suddenly, over the intercom came a shout from an after-station gunner: "Bandit, ten o'clock low!" There, low on our port side a few miles away, came an airplane, barely visible in its camouflage paint job, climbing to meet us.

Following squadron policy, I vacated the right seat to allow Lt. (jg.) Hovde in the cockpit, and hurried to the after-station blister, grabbing my Tommy gun as I passed the bunk compartment. The blister gunners were ready and the 50s were charged and ready to fire as the unknown aircraft turned and began making a pursuit curve run on us. My Tommy gun, too, was ready for action.

It was when the plane was nearing the range of our guns that I identified it, and I picked up the mike and yelled, "Hold your fire, that's a Frog Morane-Saulnier, it's no Fiat!" The French fighter sped past us, dipping its wings in salute, and turned off toward the east. It's a good thing I had built a model of a Morane-Saulnier before I joined the Navy. We very easily could have shot him down.

IOWA

For several weeks the BBC overseas broadcasts had hinted of a meeting between the Big Three: Roosevelt, Churchill and Stalin. The meeting was to be held somewhere in the Mid-East.

On November 27, 1943, my crew and I were scheduled for a coverage. Our skipper, Lt. Cdr. John Odell, and his co-pilot, Lt.

Don Hughes, would be PPCs, and Lt. (jg.) E.T.J. "Gabby" Hartnett and I would serve as second pilots and navigators. No explanation was given for the extra pilot, or of why the skipper was taking the flight.

With the take-off time set for 0300, we were in the briefing tent at 0130. It was a misty, cold morning, and the shelter of the tent felt good, though the tent surely did leak.

The briefing officer informed us that the ships we were to cover were the battleship *Iowa* and three Fletcher-class destroyers. When we plotted the position of interception of the convoy, someone remarked that it was a long way out—six hundred miles west of Agadir!

As the Air Combat Intelligence Officer finished his briefing, he said very seriously, "Now, fellows, be sure you find the ships, and don't get lost and wander all over the ocean. When your radioman makes contact with the ship, be certain he does it in a smart, seamanlike manner. There are high diplomatic officials on that battleship."

"I bet Roosevelt is on that battlewagon," I said. "I doubt it," said Commander Odell. "He'd fly over." To this I replied, "Okay, I'll bet you fifty francs Roosevelt is on that ship." We shook hands and the bet was on.

We took off at the prescribed time and headed out on course to intercept the four ships. In order to conserve fuel, we flew at an airspeed of 75 knots.

The mist, rain, and low ceiling forced us to fly at an altitude of 300 feet, just under the heavy clouds. The heaving, white-capped waves below verified our estimate of the wind; it appeared to be blowing from 090 degrees at over 40 knots.

As dawn approached and the time for the interception neared, we all became tense. Suddenly, the wait was over and the radar operator announced over the intercom, "Target dead ahead, twenty miles." All eyes strained to get a glimpse of the convoy.

First, one of the destroyers came into view. At times it seemed completely submerged as the angry green waves cascaded over it. Someone commented over the intercom that those DDs should get submariner's pay, since they were submerged so much of the time.

A few moments later the *Iowa* came into view, a huge, towering, slate-gray behemoth, charging out of the fog and mist, seemingly impervious to the turbulent ocean as it rode majestically through the roiling waves, the bow sending tons of water crashing over the gun turrets.

I imagined FDR sitting there on the bridge in his cape, content in the knowledge that VP-73 was watching over him.

We let down to 200 feet and flew alongside the *Iowa* so that our radioman would have a clear view of the bridge while he signaled with the Aldis lamp. Suddenly I realized that that battleship was going as fast as we were! The *Iowa* was churning through the sea at 35 knots; our PBY was flying at 75 knots into a 40-knot headwind, which made our speed over the ocean the same as the battleship's. We never did get ahead of the *Iowa* by very much.

The signaling done—in a smart and seamanlike manner—we continued our coverage, although, because of the distance, we were on station less than an hour.

Six hours later, after a thirteen-hour flight, we landed at Agadir. Several weeks later, after FDR was home, we found I had been right. Fifty francs equalled one dollar.

ON BEING A CO-PILOT

Ensigns Cain and Snare and I knew that we were replacements for the pilots lost when Lt. (jg.) Fuchs crashed due to engine failure on a night take-off on October 1.

We soon realized that, as new Ensigns, we were the low men on the totem pole. According to my log, I was made PPIP (Patrol Plane 1st Pilot) on December 8, 1943. Our Executive Officer, Lt. Dryden W. Hundley, was my check pilot, and he really gave me a going over. Uncle John, as we called him (when he wasn't within earshot), had been flying for many years before the war, and had been a Flying Chief prior to receiving a commission. He was a crusty soul, honest, and someone we felt confident to be flying with.

Following my three-hour check ride, I sought out the shade of the O Club, which, incidentally, had been well stocked with the booty we had brought from Puerto Rico, as you recall. There I met Ensigns Cain and Snare, and we talked over my check ride and the favorable results. As we sat sipping paper cups full of warm rum, Cain reached into his pocket, pulled out a piece of paper, and from it he read this bit of doggerel:

The Co-Pilot
I'm the co-pilot, I sit on the right.
I'm not important—just part of the flight.
I never talk back, lest I have regrets,
But I have to remember what the Captain forgets.
I make out the flight plans and study the weather,
Pull up the gear and stand by to feather,
Fill out the forms and do the reporting,
And fly the old crate when the Captain is courting.
I take all the readings, and adjust the power,
Handle the flaps and call the tower.
I find our position on the darkest of nights,
and do all of the bookwork without any lights.
I call for my Captain and buy him his Cokes,
Then I have to laugh at his corny jokes.
More than once in a while, when his landings are rusty,
I'm right on the spot with a "Gawd, ain't it gusty?"
All in all, I'm a general stooge,
As I sit to the right of this man I call "Scrooge."
I hope against hope, that with great understanding,
He'll soften a bit, and let *me* shoot a landing.

With that Jim stood up, gave a deep bow, and sat down . . . missing his chair completely! We figured he'd had enough rum for a day.

Let it never be said that we didn't get enough hours in the air. Our weekly schedule went like this:

Operational mission
Training flight (bombing, gunnery, navigation)
Duty Officer (24-hour tour) at least once a month
Day off
Ready Duty (Alert Crew)
Operational mission
Training flight

Most of the operational missions—i.e., convoy escort, A/S sweeps, air-rescue and reconnaissance flights—averaged twelve to fourteen hours in length, some even longer. The training hops were three to four hours in the air, giving all three pilots a chance to brush up on instrument flying, emergency procedures, and the necessary teamwork that a combat air crew requires for success and survival. The Patrol Plane Commanders (PPCs) aided the newer members of the pilot crew in becoming proficient in the operation of the Catalinas, with the eventual goal of the co-pilots checking out as PPCs and having crews of their own.

In VP-73 very little regard was given to rank. The only senior officer we saluted was the skipper, Lt. Cdr. Odell, and on the flight line even this military gesture was forgotten. He was addressed for the most part as "Cap'n." The other pilots, even those of higher rank, were addressed by their first names or nicknames. This casual approach to military discipline was not uncommon in the flying units, but it was rare in the black-shoe, seagoing Navy.

It was my goal to become a PPC . . . then I would be a full-fledged P-boat pilot.

SING-ALONG

"Yankee Doodle," America's Revolutionary War thumb-to-nose call to battle, contains a verse that perfectly describes the songs, ballads and parodies produced by American airmen the world over down through the years. It went like this:

"It suits for feasts, it suits for fun;
And just as well for fighting."

The pilots and air crews of VP-73, lacking even a piano at Agadir, were obliged to do their singing *a capella*. It really didn't matter, for even a full orchestra would not have improved the quality of our vocalizing.

In every military unit in all the armies and navies of the world, some tunes are more popular and sung more frequently than others. This was certainly true in VP-73. One of the most popular tunes was this one, sung to the tune of the original British original, "Troopship Leaving Bombay," or "Bless, 'Em All":

A P-boat was leaving the states,
Bound for old Agadir,
The compass was crazy, the rudder was jammed,
The pilots were drunk, and they said they'd be damned,
Oh they flew for days and for days,
Through fog and through sleet and through haze,
They raised a commotion o'er all of the ocean.
When they landed, the crew were amazed.

(Chorus): Bless them all, bless them all.
The long and the short and the tall,
Bless all the blondies and all the brunettes,
Each pilot is happy to take what he gets,
So we're giving the eye to them all,
To those who attract and apall,
Each Sally and Susie,
You can't be too choosy,
So cheer up my lads,
Bless 'em all.
I'm only an Ensign, a' flying a boat,
Over the deep blue sea,
No matter what happens, I'm always the goat,
I've a B—rd for a PPC.
We dress like the Ay-rabs and eat like the Frogs,

Down on the Wadi Sebou,
'tween standing the duty and writing the log,
There's not much else we're to do.
   (Chorus)

Another favorite was this, sung to the tune of "I Wanted Wings":

I wanted wings until I got the g—d-mned things,
Now I don't want them anymore.
They taught me how to fly, and they sent me here to die,
I've had my belly full of war.
Oh, I'm too young to die in a lousy PBY,
That's for the eager, not for me,
I don't trust my luck, getting picked up by a Duck,
After I've crashed into the sea.
I'd rather keep on drinking, than to stop this crate from sinking,
With my hand around a bottle, and not a g—d-mned throttle
Oh, I'm too young to die in a lousy PBY,
That's for the eager, not for me.

Another went in part like this:

Oh, you'll never get to Heaven in a PBY,
'cause the goldarned thing won't fly that high,
I ain't gonna grieve my Lord no more.

And then there was this one, sung to the tune of "Battle Hymn of the Republic":

By the ring around his eyeball
You can tell a bombardier.
And you can tell a P-boat pilot
By the spread across his rear.
You can tell a navigator
By his sextants, charts and such.
You can tell a fighter pilot—
But you can't tell him much!

There were, of course many, many more, but these are a few that were sung whenever the aircrews became musically inclined.

P-BOAT vs. CONDOR

Admiral Karl Dönitz, head of the German U-Bootwaffe, the submarine fleet, was seeking to make his underseas fleet more effective. Allied naval forces were slowly but surely decimating his U-boats and forcing those that remained to operate farther and farther from their bases in occupied France.

In order to increase their effectiveness, he organized them into "wolf packs" of six to twelve boats, and, working in conjunction with the Luftwaffe's Focke-Wulf 200Cs, he anticipated great carnage in the Allied convoys.

He anticipated correctly.

Lt. Edward Bourgeault was the PPC of 73-P-1, assigned to escort a British convoy of four vessels north of the Strait of Gibraltar. For several hours the coverage was uneventful. Then things changed dramatically.

The starboard waist lookout suddenly called attention to two aircraft flying very high and heading in their direction. Ed and his co-pilot, thinking they were a pair of British Wellingtons out for a look-see at the Battle of the Atlantic, decided to climb to the visitors' altitude and exchange greetings.

Still circling the convoy, Lt. Bourgeault applied throttle and headed up to meet the newcomers. As he approached the nearest plane, he saw the bomb bays open, and several dark objects plummeted towards the vessels below.

Bombs! The two intruders were not British Wellingtons, rather they were German Focke-Wulf 200 Condors, the largest long-range bomber in the Luftwaffe inventory!

Hearing the after-station report that the Focke-Wulfs' bombs had struck and damaged one of the ships in the convoy, Lt. Bourgeault put 73-P-1 in a climbing turn directly under the lead Condor, thwarting, to some extent, the bombardiers' aim on the rest of the convoy.

After what seemed like hours, the VP-73 plane reached the Focke-Wulf's altitude. Leveling off at the altitude of the enemy plane, Ed banked 73-P-1 to a collision course. The Condor also turned, and the two planes were soon coming head-on toward each other with all guns blazing.

Suddenly the German plane nosed down a little to give the upper gunners an opportunity to fire, and passed under the PBY. Lt. Bourgeault pulled the P-boat up in a wing-over, allowing the bow gunner a perfect shot with the twin 30s of the nose turret. The port waist gunner also fired a long burst from his 50-caliber into the enemy.

The dorsal gun of the Focke-Wulf fired a lethal burst into 73-P-1, wounding the two waist gunners and the ordinance man on the tunnel-gun.

With a shout over the intercom, the plane captain in the tower called everyone's attention to the smoke pouring from one engine of the Focke-Wulf. It had turned toward the coast, losing altitude, accompanied by the other Condor.

The battle was over, with VP-73's plane the victor.

Returning to the patrol altitude of eight hundred feet, Lt. Bourgeault resumed coverage of the English ships. The wounds of the injured crewmen were treated by the plane captain and navigator. At long last, 73-P-1 received permission from the Moroccan Sea Frontier to return to base with the wounded.

Before leaving the convoy, Lt. Bourgeault flew past the convoy Commander, advising him that he was leaving the coverage and requesting their position, so that the relief patrol plane could be informed.

This information was given.

As 73-P-1 pulled away from the little fleet of ships, the convoy Commander sent one last message: "Thanks for the coverage."

Several months later, Lt. Bourgeault and his crew were properly recognized for their action with the Focke-Wulfs.

CHRISTMAS 1943

This was a stupid way to have to spend Christmas Eve. Herding a plodding convoy several hundred miles off the coast of French Morocco certainly didn't bring out the yuletide spirit.

This afternoon, back at the base at Agadir, Dripps and Oberhofer hooted at us as we trudged from Operations. They were all set to go on liberty to spend Christmas Eve in town, and were decked out in their dress blues. Compared to them, we looked like a bunch of bums in our greasy, sweat-stained flight suits and ball caps.

As we helped the plane captain and the mechs pre-flight the PBY, we could see some of the fellows in their tents, turning thorn bushes into crude Christmas trees and decorating them with baubles and bangles made from cigarette wrappers and scrap metal from the salvage yard. One hut featured an aluminum tree fashioned from the radar-jamming window, then painted a startling yellow-green with zinc-chromate primer scrounged from the paint locker.

As we climbed aboard the P-boat, we saw more of the squadron boisterously boarding the dilapidated French charcoal-burning bus for Christmas Eve services at the cathedral in Agadir. I don't think they were all Catholics, but I guess they figured it was better to attend there than not at all. All nine of us felt like martyrs. Why couldn't that convoy have stayed out of our sector until the 26th? They certainly showed VP-73 no consideration.

Darkness was falling. The gray troop ships of the convoy were almost invisible in the fading light. With dusk, it was time to communicate with the convoy Commander with the Aldis lamp, to be given the speed and course the vessels would maintain throughout the night.

As our radioman blinked and counter-blinked with the leader of the convoy, my thoughts went to the GIs aboard the ships. The vessels were completely blacked out, no sign of life was visible on the equipment-laden decks. I imagined the troops below decks, lying in their tiered bunks, some asleep, some, I thought, maybe organizing a song-fest to herald in the season. Perhaps a GI Santa was working his way through the crowded holds, passing out cigarettes and candy to the soldiers, the gifts carried in a government-issue duffel bag.

Leaving the convoy, I thought about something else. What of the U-boat that Intelligence had reported in the area? It didn't seem right to torpedo a troopship on Christmas Eve, and neither did it seem Christian to sink a sub tonight. Peace on earth was a long way from our section of the Atlantic.

Perhaps the Unterseeboot would stay submerged, safely hidden by the sullen waves as its crew observed Christmas Eve. The crew was probably making do with what they had, just as we are. Maybe they were singing "O Tannenbaum" or "Stille Nacht."

Then someone brushed my right shoulder. It was our plane captain, fastening a sprig of holly to the throttles on the overhead between us. "Merry Christmas!" he yelled in our ears.

Suddenly our intercom was alive. The gunner in the after-station suggested that we sing carols. Lt. (jg.) Marshall volunteered to be song leader, and all through the night, as we flew our lonely coverage, the hull of our PBY echoed with "Joy to the World," "O, Little Town of Bethlehem," and all the others. I never knew Marsh knew all those songs.

With the coming of the dawn our vigil ended. A dot on the horizon signaled our relief. We left our station on the convoy.

As we clambered down the ladder at Agadir, all of us felt the same. That was certainly a dumb way to spend Christmas Eve.

HAPPY HOUR

Things were happening fast. Our squadron received orders transferring us from Agadir to Port Lyautey, several hundred miles north. There we would work in conjunction with VP-63 in flying barrier patrols in the Strait of Gibraltar and convoy escort for vessels entering the Mediterranean Sea from the Atlantic.

We all felt that our standard of living had improved, as at Port Lyautey we lived in Quonset huts rather than in tents, and we flew from paved runways instead of gravel and clay. We also enjoyed the luxury of a real control tower, all camouflaged with patches of green and gray paint and sporting four rows of bullet holes where a Navy F-4-F had strafed it during the invasion a year ago.

Port Lyautey was also the home base of the Headquarters Squadron (Hedron) which served all of the naval air units both in Morocco and on the Mediterranean. Aircraft overhaul, maintenance, supplies—in short, anything could be obtained from the Hedron.

Especially athletics.

When I attended Norfolk Senior High School, I was too small to go out for football. Jack Stubbs and Marv Stinebaugh would have demolished me. When I attended Wayne State Teachers College in 1940-41, my size still kept me from the gridiron. I was reluctant to allow Lowell Magdanz and Bud Best to use me for a tackling dummy.

Throughout the ordeal of pre-flight school, I had managed to survive, and, upon graduation, I confined my athletics to swimming. I figured that, since the Navy was concerned mostly with water activities, swimming would contribute much to my chances of survival. Every day, a full Lieutenant would make the rounds of the Quonsets yelling, "Happy Hour!" He was clad in a sweat suit, shorts, and black, Navy-issue high-top tennis shoes with the white circles at the ankle bones, and he always carried a football. His name was Lt. Paul William Bryant, but everyone called him Bear. Whenever he would catch me in our hut, I would always beg off. Either I had just got in from a flight, or was preparing to go on one, or I had some important reports and letters to write. The football turned me off. Had he suggested going swimming, I might have relented. But no Lt. Bryant was going to teach me how to play football. I never did join him on the crude gridiron of Port Lyautey.

Years later I had a happy reunion with Lt. Arthur N. Smith, a squadron mate of VP-73. We hadn't seen each other for almost forty years, since we flew together in Patrol Squadron 73. As we recalled the times we spent together in the Navy, we came to the subject of "whatever happened to . . . ?" It was during this reminiscing that Smitty said, "Well, you remember Bear Bryant, don't you?"

"You mean the football coach of Alabama?" I asked. "What about him?"

"He was the officer, attached to the Hedron, who used to come around every day wanting us to come out for football during the Happy Hour. Don't you remember him?"

With my memory refreshed, I did recall Lt. Bryant and my refusal to be on his football team. I am probably the only person in the whole wide world who refused to play football with Bear Bryant, who would later become one of the top football coaches in the nation.

ROOWB

There are many exclusive clubs in aviation. "Quiet Birdmen" work without fanfare in aeronautical promotions; American airmen who parachute from disabled aircraft automatically become members of the "Caterpillar Club"; and Royal Air Force pilots who were fished from the English Channel during the Battle of Britain became members of the "Goldfish."

Patrol Squadron 73 also had its select group, the "ROOWB," or "Royal Order of Whale Bangers." The Order was given to aircrews who dropped a stick of depth charges on that denizen of the deep, the whale, in the belief that they were attacking an enemy submarine.

My crew and I qualified for this prestigious award following an incident off the coast of French Morocco in 1944. We had taken off from Port Lyautey at last light for an anti-submarine sweep of the shipping lanes in the Strait of Gibraltar. After patrolling all night without incident, we anxiously awaited the dawn. All of the crew were at their stations, their eyes scanning the sea and sky. Dawn was the time when U-boats might be caught on the surface, having come up during the night to charge their batteries in relative safety from attack.

Suddenly one of the lookouts in the port blister shouted over the intercom, "Sub! Dead ahead!"

Nine sets of eyeballs strained toward the ocean ahead. There it was! A blackish shape, almost hidden by the heaving whitecaps, the angry sea swirling and breaking over what seemed to be the conning tower.

Lt. (jg.) Art Smith, my co-pilot, pressed the buzzer, sending the crew to battle stations. Navigator Lt. (jg.) Oren Marshall handed the radioman our position. Immediately, radio sent out our call sign, position and a continuous series of S's in Morse code. The S's signified that we were attacking a U-boat.

From our patrol altitude of 800 feet, we nosed down to the required bombing altitude of 100 feet. With mixtures full rich, props in high pitch and throttles full forward, we reached the attack speed of 120 knots. Ordinance reported over the intercom that all four depth charges were armed and ready.

We swept toward the awash "Unterseeboot," approaching at a slight angle to its apparent course. Inasmuch as all of our bombing was done by "seaman's eye," I held the pickle switch, my thumb ready to press the red button at the proper moment. Closer, closer, we came, then, "Bombs Away!" I felt 73-P-6 lighten as the four 325-pound depth bombs dropped from the wing racks. As they plummeted toward the target, I was flabbergasted at what I saw.

Our submarine was a whale!

Banking slightly to port, we saw the whale smack dab in the middle of the four geysers of water thrown up by the exploding depth charges. Its huge flukes whacked the ocean, then it sounded.

It was almost an hour before we could get a message through to cancel our contact report as the airwaves were full of messages of other units coming to our aid. Finally we were recalled to Port Lyautey.

A waiting staff car whisked us to the headquarters of the Moroccan Sea Frontier where we explained our actions. Hours later we were driven back to the squadron.

All of VP-73 was on hand to welcome us. The skipper came

forward and handed Smitty, Marsh and me aluminum silhouettes of whales cut from scrap metal. On each was crudely stamped "ROOWB." With proper dignity and some biting sarcasm he inducted us into the Royal Order of Whale Bangers.

I wonder what that old whale thought?

TORPEDOES

In the fall I was named a PPC (Patrol Plane Commander) after a check ride with Lt. Hundley, our Executive Officer. "Uncle John" was a strict taskmaster, and when he gave an "up" on a check ride, you knew you had made a real accomplishment.

The day after I had been made PPC and received my full instrument ticket, Patrol Squadron 73 received some exciting news. All flights had been canceled, and we were to stand by for further information. As we clustered around the Operations Quonset, we observed trucks from Ordinance pulling up to our PBYs towing long bomb-like objects—torpedoes! They were hanging them on our P-boats.

After what seemed like a lifetime, the skipper emerged from Operations and he briefed us on what was happening. He told us that a French Resistance coast-watcher had reported to the British Office of Naval Intelligence that what appeared to be a German battleship had slipped out of occupied France through the Bay of Biscay and was headed for the southern convoy routes. We were to stand by until further information was received. If the report were true and the Nazis' battleship appeared in our area, we were to torpedo it!

Torpedo a heavily armed German battleship from a PBY? What were they thinking?

None of us had ever launched a live torpedo from a PBY. We had dropped inert cement-filled dummies in operational training, but none of us had even seen a real one.

If this alert were true, I thought, the Japanese kamikazes we were beginning to hear about would have nothing on us. We'd be blasted out of the sky before we could launch the fish. We didn't stand a chance—that we knew.

Yet, in spite of these misgivings, all of the squadron went about preparing for the possibility of torpedoing a German battlewagon.

The Air Combat Intelligence (ACI) officers were poring over lead models of German battleships, trying to determine the best angle of attack. The Ordinance Department had somewhere resurrected a dozen torpedo directors, a device mounted on the instrument panel at eye level with the co-pilot. A sight located on the protractor-like top allowed the proper degree of lead to be determined. The first pilots of each crew were grouped around the ordinance men, getting last-minute instructions on the use of the sight. Across the field we could see ambulances with their Red Cross markings lining up before the base hospital. We didn't like to contemplate those preparations.

The busiest of all were the chaplains. Once the various briefings on the uses of the equipment were completed, each aircrew sought out the tent of their chaplain, who led them in special services dealing with the 23rd Psalm. There would be no atheists in the Catalinas of VP-73 that day.

Church services over, the airmen dispersed. Some sat on fuel drums and wrote letters home; some, with great animation, attempted an air of bravado; others just sat, deep in their own thoughts.

After standing by for what seemed an eternity, the alert was canceled. Evidently the coast-watcher was in error. No German battleships were loose on the high seas. All of VP-73 heaved a sigh of relief as the order was given to stand down. Though we were not required to make torpedo runs on any battleship, I am convinced that every aircrew would have done its best, and all would have made the attack. On that day, the corpsmen and doctors conducting "sick call" reported that *no one* had reported in to them with any ailment, real or imagined.

OPEN-SEA LANDING

Patrol Squadron 73 was justly proud of the fact that, of the hundreds of ships escorted through U-boat-infested waters and in the thousands of hours flown in the coverage, not a single vessel under its protection was sunk or even attacked by the undersea raiders.

The sector of the Atlantic under the squadron's jurisdiction was vast. It extended six hundred miles west of Port Lyautey, French Morocco, south to the Canary Islands, then east to the tiny Spanish province of Ifni on the West African coast. The sector below was covered by the British Sunderland squadron based at Port Étienne.

Though we were land-based, we regularly practiced water landings on the smooth water of the breakwater-protected bay of the port city. Few of us, however, had ever made a landing in the open sea.

A lifeboat adrift changed that. It was then my crew experienced a landing in mid-Atlantic, far from the protection of a wave-smoothing breakwater.

A trawler had notified the MSF (Moroccan Sea Frontier) that they had sighted a large lifeboat adrift some five hundred miles west of Mogodor, French Morocco. The canvas cover completely hid the interior of the boat, and the trawler's crew was unable to determine if anyone was aboard. They were reluctant to heave to, as they were in known submarine-infested waters and feared a torpedo.

My crew, in 73-P-7, was in the area on an anti-submarine sweep when MSF was informed of the lifeboat. Aware of our position, the Sea Frontier ordered us to investigate the derelict, determine whether it contained any seamen and, if so, to rescue them and to sink the lifeboat so that it would not be a hazard to navigation.

After completing one leg of our search pattern, we found the lifeboat. Because of the taut canvas cover we were unable to determine whether it contained any occupants, so co-pilot Bert Hovde and I decided we would land near it and send a boarding party to determine if anyone was under the canvas.

The sea force was running about three, with long rollers heaving the waves at right angles to the 10-knot wind. Had it not been for the rollers, the sea would have been calm.

After receiving acknowledgement from all of 73-P-7's stations that they were ready for landing, we lowered the wing-tip floats, put the props in high pitch, retarded the throttles and began our letdown cross-wind and parallel to the rollers. The lifeboat was but a few hundred yards away.

Holding the PBY off the water, we maintained our altitude, just skimming the tops of the waves. As a roller heaved up under our keel, we chopped the throttles, pulled the nose up, and settled with a *rattlety-bang!* on the water. A full stall landing on water sounded as though tons of gravel were being cascaded against the metal of the hull.

With engines idling and both sea anchors streaming aft, 73-P-7 was held in position while two of the crew broke out a raft, inflated it and tossed it from the port blister. Wearing their Mae Wests, they paddled toward the lifeboat after making certain they had the right bearing to the target.

If you want to feel infinitesimal, try sitting in a PBY in mid-ocean with twenty-foot rollers heaving you up on their tops, then down below their crests, leaving you completely engulfed on all sides by angry, gray-green water. That was the most lonesome feeling I have ever experienced.

Firing Very cartridges into the air so the crew could find their way to the plane we led them back, where they reported no one aboard the lifeboat. They said they had chopped holes in it so that it would sink.

With all stations ready, we turned 73-P-7 to a cross-wind position, waited for the roller to lift us on its crest, and applied power as the wave lifted us. With both of us holding the yoke to our chests, the P-boat stormed through the heaving waves, and suddenly we were on the step, our keel lifted from the sea, and we were in the air and homeward bound!

After that landing, I fully appreciated the vastness of the sea.

Part V: 1944

16 January 1944—Squadron transfers to U.S. Naval Air Station Floyd Bennett Field, New York, N.Y.
24 April 1944—Plane 73-P-1, on detached duty at NAS Beaufort, South Carolina, crashes on take-off. Lt. Cdr. J.E. Odell, Jr., and eight crew members survive with minor injuries.
1 October 1944—Squadron designation changed from VP-73 to VPB-73.

NAS FLOYD BENNETT

The Random House *College Dictionary* has a definition for it: S CUTTLEBUTT (skut´l but´), n. 1. Naut. a. an open cask containing drinking water. b. a drinking fountain for use by the crew of a vessel. 2. Informal. rumor; gossip.

The United States Navy during World War II thrived on it. Whenever either officers or enlisted men gathered, someone always came forth with the WORD. It could be about promotions, a change of duty, who was obliged to get married—anything, no matter how remote, that might have a bearing on the well-being of the crew, the ship, the squadron, the Navy or even the Universe. The one with the WORD was always in demand, and he held forth like a courtier, dispensing his often-faulty information to any who would hearken to his WORDS.

As 1944 wore on, scuttlebutt became the order of the day.

We were being transferred to the Azores.

Our squadron was being reassigned to Rio de Janeiro.

Our PBYs were to be replaced by PB4Y-2s.

Some even had the WORD on the WORD.

At long last, the truth came out, and we were informed officially that we were being returned to the States, reassigned to NAS Floyd Bennett Field in New York.

In order to expedite the movement of the squadron, it was decided to fly the Catalinas to New York rather than send them on a seaplane tender. Though we all hoped to be among the aircrews to fly home, this was impossible because of the number of planes involved. We drew straws, and I was among those selected to return to the United States by ship.

While the men selected to fly home readied their planes and gear for the return, the rest of us boarded Navy buses for the trip to

Casablanca, where the Army Transport *General A.E. Anderson* awaited us.

We were very interested to see the huge Missouri-class French battleship *Jean Bart* lying about three hundred feet off-shore, its keel resting on the bottom of Casablanca harbor, sunk there by American torpedoes during Operation Torch. It was now used by the Free French Navy as an Annapolis-like military school, and a pontoon bridge connected it with the shore.

We stared in wonderment, too, at a French ocean liner that lay on its side with its gigantic funnel resting on the dock, enabling one to look down into the funnel's black interior.

In addition to the fifteen pilots of VP-73, the ship's passengers included eighty officers who had commanded LSTs at Salerno and were now being reassigned, and some three thousand French naval Cadets being sent to the United States for further training.

Once the *A.E. Anderson* was at sea, all of the LST officers were given duties, gun watches, officer-of-the-deck duty and all sorts of watches, as though they were regular members of the ship's company. The VP-73 officers were completely left out of any collateral duties; evidently they figured we didn't know a fantail from a porthole, and it was easier to ignore us.

Fearing that I would make a fool out of myself and become seasick, I wisely sought out Ship's Service and purchased two cartons of Hershey bars, stopped at the ship's library and checked out four books, and returned to my bunk and remained there for nine days, with very little time out of my bunk. I did not get seasick, but I did tire of the chocolate bars.

The troopship docked in New York, and Navy buses took us to NAS Floyd Bennett Field in Brooklyn. Once we were checked into our BOQ and the men were checked into their barracks, I sought out the Red Cross office to send a telegram home. The wire I sent read: "BASED IN NEW YORK. ROOF OF MOUTH SUNBURNED." When my mother read this wire, she exclaimed excitedly, "Oh! Bob's been in a crash! He's badly burned!" My brother Orv reread the letter, and handed it to her, laughing. "No, he's been gaping open-mouthed at the tall buildings, like any yokel from Nebraska would do. He's never seen a skyscraper," he said.

1944

BLIMP

Flying anti-submarine patrols and escorting convoys over the North Atlantic during the winter presented more problems than flying those same missions off the coast of Africa. The main difference, of course, was the weather. Sleet, snow, freezing rain and ice combined with mist and fog to make our flights miserable. And there had been no blimps in Morocco.

Lt. (jg.) Frank Bolin of Kansas City and I were being briefed for a convoy escort one cold, rainy morning in February of 1944. We were to escort four tankers, whose position was 150 nautical miles southeast of the Ambrose Lightship. They were to join a larger convoy further out to sea. During the briefing, the ACI officer informed us that there were no blimps in the area. To us P-boat pilots this information was very important, for the lighter-than-air craft flew at the same altitude we flew—800 feet—and in poor visibility such as we were experiencing this morning, it was vital to know their whereabouts, because the blimps were the same color as the fog.

Assured that 73-P-9 would have the sky to itself, we took off from Floyd Bennett and headed for the convoy. At 800 feet we were just under the scudding overcast, and fog reduced our visibility to a quarter of a mile. As we neared the convoy's plotted position, all stations were alert, anxious to see whose eyes were the keenest.

Suddenly the intercom clicked and an excited voice rang in our ears, "Afterstation to pilot; Sir, there's something dead ahead, blue lights!" The voice shouted. Frank and I saw the light, and, as though we had practiced the maneuver for years, pulled the yoke back to our chests, twisted the wheels to the left and performed a perfect chandelle. Luckily we both spun the wheels in the same direction. As we leveled out, heading away from the object, the afterstation informed us, "Sir, that's a blimp. We almost rammed it!"

We were nonplused. With a blimp doing the coverage, there was no need for our presence. Why was the blimp out, when the

ACI officer said none would be patrolling in our area today? Were we or they, through an error in navigation, covering the wrong convoy?

Seeking an answer, we flew away from the convoy with the blimp covering it and sent a message to base: "Blimp over convoy. Request instructions."

A message from our base dit-dahed in our radioman's ears. "No blimps in area. What is your position?"

Heading warily back to the convoy-escorting blimp, we slowly flew by it as our radioman blinked with the Aldis lamp a request for the blimp's position. Its position was immediately flashed to us. With a "Roger" to the blimp, we flew low past the convoy Commander and requested by Aldis lamp their position. Receiving it, we compared the three plots, ours and the two others, and found they all coincided, give or take a mile or so. Our navigation was not at fault; we were over the correct group of tankers.

A message rang in our radioman's ears: "Return to base."

Leaving the convoy and its patrolling airship, we headed back to Floyd Bennett, where we were met by two staff cars from the headquarters of the Eastern Sea Frontier at 90 Church Street. The officer-in-charge told us to bring all of our charts, logs and notes and to accompany him to ESF headquarters. Our skipper, aware of the affair, whispered to us to stand our ground, that he was behind us.

We were grilled; our charts, logs and notes were scrutinized; and finally we were returned to Floyd Bennett without being apprised of any decision.

Several weeks later, our skipper informed us that there was *no blimp* over the convoy. He told us he thought some officer at 90 Church Street forgot to inform ACI of the blimp. The officer had too much rank to be wrong. As a result, we junior officers took the blame.

Frank and I both agreed that they sure would have been surprised if we had bumped into the blimp that wasn't there.

1944

COAST GUARD

Many of the pilots of VP-73 envied the pilots of the Coast Guard unit based with them at Floyd Bennett. The Catalina pilots had only one type of aircraft to fly, while the Coast Guardsmen had several—the Grumman JRF-5 Goose, the big Hall-Aluminum PH-3s and their recently acquired Sikorsky YR-4 helicopters.

Trials were being conducted to determine the practicality of landing the YR-4s on the fantail of a merchant ship, with the ultimate goal of using them as a self-contained anti-submarine weapon. In a remote area of Floyd Bennett a platform was erected, mounted on hydraulic pistons that caused the structure to pitch and heave much as a ship would do in rough seas. The Coast Guard pilots spent hours practicing landing on the bucking mock-up of a merchant ship's fantail landing pad, and eventually became very adept at the task.

One afternoon Lt. (jg.) William "Joker" Joachim and I were returning from an anti-submarine sweep in 73-P-4. Ensign Thompson was in the navigation compartment and was feeling well-satisfied with himself for getting us back to Floyd Bennett right on the ETA.

As we entered the traffic pattern over the waters of Jamaica Bay adjacent to Floyd Bennett, we noticed what appeared to be a teenaged boy standing forlornly on a small sandbar some five hundred yards offshore. With the tide out, several small islands could be seen, but in a few hours they would all be under water again.

As we flew over him, the boy waved, and it was then we noticed that no boat was in sight. We could see that he had a tackle box and fishing pole on the sand beside him.

As I circled the islet, Joker called Floyd Bennett tower and informed them of the boy and that he seemed to be marooned. Perhaps they had better send someone out to investigate, he suggested.

The tower agreed with us, and asked us to drop a float light or smoke bomb so that the rescuers could pinpoint the proper sandbar. We kept circling the boy, we dropped both a float light and smoke bomb, then waited for the rescuer. The boy kept waving to us.

Suddenly we saw one of the Coast Guard's YR-4 helicopters come swooping into sight. With its rotor sparkling in the sun, it flew to the smoke-marked islet, and as the boy cowered at the edge of the water away from the whirling rotor, the Coast Guard pilot landed and motioned the lad to come over to him. We could see the boy get into the machine. They then rose vertically into the air, and sped off to Floyd Bennett. We stopped circling, and returned to the base and landed. That evening we were told by the Coast Guard pilot the full story of the boy on the sandbar. The boy and his pal had gone fishing that morning, using a rowboat to get to the sandbar. Fishing was good—so good, in fact, that the boys ran out of bait. One of the boys took the boat back to shore to get the needed supplies. When these had been obtained and he returned to the boat, he saw that the wind had come up, making the waters of Jamaica Bay very rough and hazardous. Rather than risk rowing to his pal on the sandbar, he pulled the boat up on the shore and went home, leaving his friend marooned. The youthful Robinson Crusoe had been on the spit several hours when we arrived over him.

The Coast Guard pilots were very excited about the flight. They told us it was the first time a helicopter had been used for an actual rescue mission, and they were pleased with the way everything worked.

Joker and I were just as tickled over the whole affair as the Coast Guard pilots were, but we were concerned about one thing: What did the maroonee say to the marooner when next they met?

BOMBS AWAY

As spring of 1944 came, reports of increased U-boat activity south of our New York sector reached the Eastern Sea Frontier. In order to increase the coverage, ESF detached three of our planes to NAS Beaufort, South Carolina. Our skipper, Lt. Cdr. John Odell, lead the unit.

For several days the missions of anti-submarine sweeps and convoy escort were carried out uneventfully. Then, on April 24,

1944

Cdr. Odell and his crew in 73-P-1 were scheduled for a night mission, with a 2100 departure time. As 73-P-1 left the runway promptly at 2100, the starboard engine backfired, and abruptly stopped. The PBY was then only two hundred feet in the air, with the landing gear still down. The crew fought to keep the plane in level flight with the one engine out, and full port rudder was applied. The ship wallowed through the air, unable to keep flying with 1,275 gallons of fuel aboard. Immediately Cdr. Odell pulled the red bomb release handle and jettisoned the four 325-pound torpex-filled depth charges.

The Catalina slammed into the marshy ground some two miles from the departure spot. The extended gear held for a few yards, until the port wheel hit a tree stump, sheared and caused the plane to slew around, tearing off the wing and rupturing the fuel tanks. Cdr. Odell and the other eight men in the crew successfully evacuated the crushed PBY just as the fuel exploded. No one was seriously injured.

As the salvage crew surveyed the burnt wreckage the next morning, a whiskery tenant farmer approached the Navy men and said, "Suhs, I'se sho sorry that airyplane got all burnt up on this here propitty of mine and I ain't gwine to charge you for trespassin, but ah shore would be mighty beholdent to you all if you'd get that big bomb outta my house." One of the bombs had burrowed through the marsh, coming to rest under the floor of the farmer's kitchen!

Things had hardly calmed down after the skipper's crash at Beaufort than we had another bomb-related incident at Floyd Bennett.

For practice bombing we used small cast iron missiles weighing about five pounds. Special blank shells were inserted in the bombs which emitted a flash of light and a puff of white smoke when it hit the water. Tube-like racks held the forty-eight practice bombs, twenty-four under each wing. Each time a bombing run was made, two projectiles were dropped, spaced by the intervalometer of the Norden sight in the bow of the plane. The spacing was roughly 260 feet from the first bomb to the second, the lethal area of four depth charges. The target was usually a towed sled pulled by a speedy crash boat that simulated the wash of a submarine. To score a hit, the puffs of smoke of the impact must be on each side of the target—a straddle.

As one of our planes returned from a practice mission, it had to fly over the tenements of Brooklyn. One of the iron bombs had not dropped, but was hung up in the bomb rack. Since it had not released in all of this time the crew did not fear it releasing now over densely populated Flatbush Avenue. How wrong they were. Over mid-Brooklyn the bomb shook loose and plummeted toward the ground below. The aircrew watched helplessly as it fell.

Upon landing, the crew dutifully reported the mishap, then stood by for any repercussions. None seemed to be forthcoming. But a few days later, the Commanding Officer of Floyd Bennett received a letter from the super (superintendent) of a building on Flatbush Avenue. The letter stated that the bomb had hit his building, penetrated six floors, and came to rest in the bathroom of his apartment, where it hit his false teeth, which stood at the time in a water glass on the toilet tank. He stated he was willing to do all of the repairs himself without charge to the Navy as part of his contribution to the war effort; but, he said, he wished the Navy would pay for his false teeth. This they did immediately.

It was lucky the teeth were in the water glass and not in his head.

LEND LEASE

Despite the saying "Don't volunteer for anything," sixty-nine air crews from patrol squadrons of the Atlantic Fleet volunteered to ferry aircraft to the Soviets under Lend Lease.

In August of 1944 my crew, Lt. Martin Najarian, Lt. (jg.) A.N. Smith and I, along with our plane captain, radiomen and ordinance men arrived in Elizabeth City, North Carolina, where we were told that we were to deliver 138 PBN-1 Nomads to the Soivietsky Soyuz Morskaya Aviatsiya, the Soviet Naval Air Force. The PBN was built in the Naval Aircraft Factory in Philadelphia, and was an improved version of the Consolidated-built PBY Catalinas we had been flying. It was strictly a flying boat, however, and had no landing gear.

Upon arriving at the base, we were ushered to the air station auditorium, where, after an American briefing officer explained our purpose, a bemedalled Russian colonel took over the rostrum. His opening remarks were, "I want you all to know that these airplanes belong to the Union of Soviet Socialist Republics."

Everybody nudged the fellow beside him. We were under the impression that the U.S. was "loaning" the planes to the Reds, and this guy was claiming full ownership even before we had delivered them.

The colonel then proceeded to read the aircraft operating manual to us in Russian, and it was translated back into English by an American sailor translator. The whole thing was ridiculous, as we were all familiar with the aircraft and were not about to abuse them.

Once the Russian had had his say, the American briefing officer told us that we were to take the planes to Kodiak, Alaska, and since they would bear Russian markings and lettering, we were to profess ignorance if we should be asked the significance of the markings.

Though we all three were PPCs, Naj, who outranked us, assumed the leadership of all of us.

In improving the PBY design, the PBN factory added two steps to the hull to improve the plane's take-off characteristics. As a result, the plane would get up on the step quicker and become airborne much faster. These steps also caused the plane to skip and bounce fantastically high into the air if the plane contacted the water at too great a speed.

Smitty and I didn't seem to have too much trouble, but the landings that Naj made were something to behold!

Our flight to Kodiak went smoothly enough, although we did have to use Lake Ponchartrain near New Orleans as an alternate landing spot. As we were on the water there, a cluster of civilians rowed over to us in small boats, and we had to ignore their questions about the Russian markings on the planes.

During the flight to Kodiak all of the crews found it necessary to delve into the inventory of supplies on the planes. Pads of paper and pencils were used by the radiomen and navigators, everybody had some of the candy bars, and the coffee was a welcome addition to our sandwiches.

Upon arrival at Kodiak we turned the planes over to the Russians. They refused to accept a single one of them! They demanded that the inventories be complete, and would not accept them until all of the candy bars and coffee canisters were replaced, along with the pads of paper and pencils. The replacement had to be of the same brand as we had used, and you can imagine the trouble the American Project Officer was caused by their demands.

Our second trip to Kodiak was without incident; none of us used a single item from the ship's inventories. No one was anxious to create another international incident over anything as strategic as coffee, candy bars, pencils and pads of paper!

Of the many landings we made during the two trips, Naj still made the most spectacular ones. I never realized a flying boat could bounce that high and still hold together. We had quite a time reminding Naj of the gremlins that caused him to bounce every landing.

LEIGH LIGHT

The night belonged to the U-boats.

The undersea raiders surfaced under the cover of darkness to recharge their batteries, and with the aid of their excellent Zeiss 7x50 binoculars, they were able to penetrate the darkness well enough to evade most prowling anti-submarine vessels. Their speed on the surface, being greater than that of most of the convoys they stalked, enabled them to attack at the most favorable time, causing great havoc.

The British came up with two airborne devices that, in combination, succeeded so well in detecting U-boats on the surface that they veritably took the night away from the Ubootwaffe. The first was the Leigh light, a twenty-four-inch searchlight devised for placement in the lower turret of a Wellington bomber by Squadron Leader Humphrey de Vere Leigh, RAF. These lights, and, later, more powerful ones of U.S. design, enabled aircraft to sight surfaced boats, especially when used in tandem with airborne microwave radar equipment (ASV). In 1943, ASV- and Leigh-equipped aircraft achieved near-total control of the ocean's surface and made the Bay of Biscay, in particular, a killing sea.

In the fall of 1944, it was decided to equip our PBYs with Leigh lights. Six crews were to be assigned night-flying duty using the three-million-candle-power searchlights. Quonset Point Naval Air Station, Rhode Island, was the location of our training base.

Lt. Ed Bourgeault (of Condor fame), Lt. (jg.) Oren Marshall and I made up one of the crews. At first we made daylight flights in the Block Island area to become familiar with the newly installed equipment. The Leigh light's electrical power source came from a dozen large batteries located under the navigation table. A carbon arc supplied by two electrodes provided the illumination. The light itself was mounted outboard of the depth charges on the starboard wing. It was thirty inches in diameter and was mounted in a streamlined housing. The switch for turning the light on was operated by the pilot, while the co-pilot controlled the direction, aiming the light by means of grips not unlike bicycle handlebars. The beam could be directed port or starboard, up or down.

In operation, the patrol would be flown at eight hundred feet above the water. In the event the ASV radar picked up a target, the pilot would be notified, and the plane would immediately dive to an altitude of one hundred feet and, with the aid of radar, home onto the blip. At a range of one mile the light was turned on and the target illuminated, the co-pilot keeping the pencil-like beam directed on it. Once the light was turned on, the pilot no longer flew by instruments, but by visual reference. Aided by the beam, he flew over the intruder and dropped his four depth charges by seaman's eye. In theory, the U-boat crew manning the conning tower and flak guns would be blinded by the intensely brilliant light and would offer no counter-fire.

Ed, Marsh and I alternated in all of the positions—navigator, pilot-bombardier and Leigh light operator—and became quite proficient.

One flight did supply a real thrill for all of us. Ed was acting as PPC and doing the flying; I was co-pilot, operating the searchlight; Marsh was in the nav comparment helping radar home us in on the target. We dropped down to one hundred feet over the water, and, one mile from the target, Ed switched on the light. As I directed the beam to find the object on the sea, I got vertigo! The cockpit, its instruments, and everything about me spun like a top. Even though the instruments on the panel showed we were in level flight, my eyes refused to believe it, and I twisted and turned in my dizziness.

Thank goodness, Ed was flying and was not affected. We continued our run, pulled up and prepared for another simulated attack. That was the only time I ever experienced vertigo.

TASSEL TESS

For two weeks the crews assigned to searchlight training had been flying five to six hours every night, making low-altitude attack runs on everything that floated near Block Island. We were all becoming very proficient at straddling our targets with practice bombs.

We did get to go ashore one weekend. "Going ashore" is Navy talk for getting some time off.

Stiff breezes blew a great deal of driftwood into our landing area (we were flying off the water at this time), and the Operations Officer canceled all water drills until the debris could be cleared. As a result, we received some time off.

Inasmuch as Boston was nearby and Lt. Bourgeault was from Boston, Ed suggested we visit his old hometown. Marsh and I thought that was a good idea, so we hitched a ride in a Navy staff car headed that way. Once in Boston, under Ed's guidance we hired a taxi for a tour of the town.

1944

After a tour of the cultural spots of Boston, Ed suggested we see if we could find his old friend, Tassel Tess. We were agreeable to that, too. In a run-down section near the waterfront, on one of Boston's narrowest streets, Ed elatedly exclaimed, "Ha, she's still here." He was referring to a decrepit bar named Flo's Cafe Exceptionale.

We cautiously went in, and although it was early in the morning, the place was jumping with sailors, merchant seamen, and waterfront characters. Marsh and I hoped we'd be able to get out with whole skins, but Ed assured us that we were as safe as if we were in church.

Some church, we thought.

All at once, a seedy-looking individual in a zoot suit mounted the stage back of the bar and announced proudly that the person we were all there to see was about to make her appearance: Tassel Tess. The bar exploded with cheers, whistles and applause.

Accompanied by a ruffle of drums from one of the orchestra members (seedy-looking, too), Tassel Tess strode from the back of the stage. She was a bleached-blond of uncertain years, wearing very little in the way of a costume. On each of her fronts, fastened to a pasty, hung a fringed tassel. Another was affixed to a jewel in her naval, and a fourth dangled from her g-string. As she turned around, she showed two more tassels mysteriously fastened to her *empennage*.

After a few remarks to some of the seamen, Tassel Tess nodded to the musicians, and the show was on.

To the tune of "Anchors Aweigh," Tess began to gyrate and writhe; then as the crowd roared its approval, the tassels began to twirl. The top ones in front whirled at high rpms, one going to the port, the other to starboard. The one on the navel jewel spun to the starboard, and the one lower down whirled to the port. When she turned around, the two on her tail were both spinning, each in a different direction. All of this going on at the same time.

She was an artiste.

At long last "Anchors Aweigh" came to an end, the tassels slowed in their spinning, and like the propellers of a switched-off

Pratt and Whitney, they came to a halt. The applause and cheering was deafening, and we joined in, wholeheartedly.

Both Marsh and I thanked Ed for exposing us to this bit of Boston culture, and reluctantly we returned to the mundane life of Naval Aviators.

Part VI: 1945

9 January 1945—Invasion of Luzon begins. B-25s of 5th Air Force, AAC, pound Clark Field.

24 January 1945—Plane 73-P-12. Lt. (jg.) L.E. Smith, USN, after a 0537 take-off experiences starboard engine failure and, in attempting to land on Jamaica Bay, crashes at 0610. Two pilots and two crew members are lost. Six members of the flight crew survive.

7 May 1945—Unconditional surrender of Germany to the Western Allies and Russia at Rheims, France.

7 May 1945—German submarine U-235 surrenders off Cape May, New Jersey.

29 May 1945—VPB-73 flies to San Juan, Puerto Rico, to fly ASR for redeploying Army Air Corps units.

6 August 1945—First atomic bomb dropped on Hiroshima, Japan.

15 August 1945—Cessation of hostilities with Japan.

MR. HAY

In early 1945 I met Mr. T. Park Hay. He was the father of my brother Frank's fiancee and was an executive of Campbell-Ewald, a large advertising agency in New York City. Mr. Hay personally handled the advertising accounts of many aviation corporations, including Eastern Airlines, which was headed by the famous World War I ace of aces, Captain Eddie Rickenbacker.

One day, as I visited with Mr. Hay, our discussion turned to the ordeal Rickenbacker had gone through when he crashed in the Pacific while a passenger in a B-17, and the three weeks of suffering that he and the survivors had endured before being rescued.

"I'm having lunch with Eddie next week," remarked Mr. Hay. "Would you like to come along and meet him?"

No question was ever answered more quickly. "You bet I would," I said, "provided I don't have to go out and fight the war."

Mr. Hay explained to me that he was a personal friend of the famous flier, and that his daughter, Dorothy Sue, and Mrs. Rickenbacker worked together in Bundles for Britain and other patriotic organizations for the war effort. The date was set; I was to meet the famous aviator and have lunch with him.

Even though my portion of the squadron was assigned Black Cat duties with the searchlight, we were still obliged to stand Ready Duty with the daylight fliers. On the day appointed for my meeting with Captain Rickenbacker, my flight crew was assigned to this Alert Crew duty. The duty would end at noon, which would still give me plenty of time to keep the luncheon date with Mr. Hay and Captain Eddie.

A few minutes before our alert duty ended, the phone in the Operations Room jangled. A U-boat had been sighted by a trawler a few hundred miles off Cape May. We had fifteen minutes to get airborne.

As we dashed to our plane, I asked one of my friends to call Mr. Hay and tell him I had to go out and fight the war, and couldn't keep the date.

We found no U-boat when we arrived at the position of the supposed sighting, and hours later we landed at Floyd Bennett.

The next day I called Mr. Hay to explain and apologize for missing our appointment. He, of course, understood, and invited me to stop at his office whenever I had my next day off, as he had a present for me from Captain Eddie.

Days later, I got to the offices of Campbell-Ewald. As I entered his suite, Mr. Hay met me and handed me a book.

It was S*even Came Through,* the book that the famous flier had written following his twenty-one days adrift in the South Pacific.

"Look inside," advised Mr. Hay.

On the inside cover was written, "With my best wishes to Lt. Robert Carlisle. Captain Eddie Rickenbacker, 1945."

The report from the trawler had spoiled the chance of a lifetime. If only the sighting had been delayed but a few minutes, I'd have been able to keep the date. I never got another.

L.E. SMITH

Ever since Eugene Ely flew off the battleship *Birmingham* over the waters of Hampton Roads, Virginia, the Navy had pilots who were not officers. They were the APs (Aviation Pilots). Most of them held the rating of Chief, and they flew in all of the squadrons in the Fleet. Admiral Byrd's pilot on his trans-Atlantic flight and over the North Pole was an AP, Floyd Bennett, after whom NAS Floyd Bennett was named. With their experience and knowledge, the Flying Chiefs were a great asset to the Navy.

After Pearl Harbor, the status of the Flying Chiefs changed dramatically. With the increase of pilots commissioned at Pensacola

1945

and Corpus Christi, hundreds of brand-new Ensigns reached the squadrons. There was very little conflict between the new Ensigns and the APs in the VF, VO/VS, VSB, and VT units. The trouble arose in the patrol and transport squadrons. Newly commissioned Ensigns were found to be reluctant to take orders from the enlisted pilots, even though the Chiefs were Patrol Plane Commanders in the VP squadrons, or Plane Commanders in the transport command. Realizing this situation existed, the Navy, in about 1943, offered commissions to those APs who desired to become officers. In VPB-73 we had two APs, Dwight McGinnis and L.E. Smith; they were both commissioned as Lieutenants, junior grade.

I flew several times with L.E. before he was commissioned, and, fully appreciating his experience, I liked flying with him, though I could sense some resentment toward me because I was an officer and had a lot to learn. But his attitude changed very little once he was commissioned a jaygee, so many of us stayed away from him to eliminate any trouble. L.E. was one of the pilots who elected to go to Quonset Point for Leigh light training. At Quonset Point, he mellowed, and during our non-flying hours all of us spent many enjoyable times in his room in the BOQ, talking and discussing everything that pilots talk about when they gather.

In mid-January we returned to Floyd Bennett.

On January 24, 1945, L.E. and his crew in 73-P-12 were scheduled for an anti-submarine sweep. 73-P-12 took off at 0537. As they climbed into the black sky, the starboard engine backfired a few times, lost power and completely failed. Turning back to Floyd Bennett, and confident that he was high enough for a landing at the field, Lt. (jg.) Smith lowered the landing gear. The drag from the extended gear was too much for the laboring port engine, and at 0610, 73-P-12 plunged into the inky water of Jamaica Bay, several miles short of Floyd Bennett's runway.

Crash boats alerted by Floyd Bennett tower sped to the scene, and though they had some difficulty in locating the plane in the darkness, they finally reached it. The entire bow of the ship, from the pylon forward, was gone. L.E. and his co-pilot were missing, as were the radioman and one of the mechanics. Six members of the crew survived. The plane captain crawled out the small window in the pylon and swam to safety. (He later attempted to crawl out of another PBY's pylon window, but was unable to squeeze through it.) All of the bodies were recovered a few days later.

The squadron was devastated by the tragedy. And things were not made any easier by the placing of the shattered 73-P-12 on the seawall near our hangar, a grim reminder of the hazards of a night take-off in a fully loaded airplane.

I shall never forget the change in Lt. (jg.) L.E. Smith. It was as though he had a premonition. Maybe he did.

COLLATERAL DUTY

All of the pilots in the squadron were assigned duties in addition to being P-boat pilots. Some were Maintenance Officers, Flight Officers, Training Officers, Navigation Officers, Armament Officers or Personnel Officers.

I was assigned to the Personnel Office; why, I don't know.

As a Personnel Officer I did find it very interesting when the PBY engaged in the battle with the Spanish Fiat. I wrote many letters to the Navy Department concerning the awarding of Purple Hearts and Air Medals. The Navy Department was reluctant to bestow the awards because Spain was not an "enemy." Wording of the citation, "With hostile enemy aircraft" turned the trick.

One cold night in February the station Duty Officer, during one of his inspections of the base, came upon one of our men siphoning gasoline from a salamander, a powered engine preheater used to warm the Pratt & Whitneys before a flight. The Duty Officer called the shore patrol and placed our man under arrest and hauled him off to the brig.

The next morning, the skipper called me in to his office, and said the base Commander had ordered a Captain's mast for the culprit. That's a type of court martial. I was to escort the miscreant to the administration building, where the mast would be held. We were to take the car owned by the lad to the court.

1945

Obtaining permission to take custody of the young fellow, we got into his car and started for the administration building. As we pulled away from the curb, the sailor said, "I sure hope we've got enough gas to get there." "Why?" I said. "You must have filled it last night from the salamander, and it should have plenty of fuel."

"Nope," he said, "while I was waiting for the Duty Officer to go to the hangar and call the shore patrol, I punched a bunch of holes in my car's gas tank so it would all leak out and they couldn't prove I'd used aviation fuel."

"I hope we've got enough to get to the ad building," I said. "Besides, if they have to test the fuel, there's enough in the lines to check."

We had plenty of fuel, and arrived at the base Commander's office. We were ushered into the Commander's plush suite, and I was curious to see what would happen now. This was the first Captain's mast I had ever attended, so I just sat and watched.

The arresting Duty Officer went over the charges, and described how the young sailor had been apprehended. Then the Commander took over. He patiently explained the charges to the boy and the evils of stealing. Then he really launched into the wages of sin, and soon the poor sailor was ready to confess everything.

So was I.

Anyway, the poor sailor started crying and explained why he had stolen the gasoline. He said he was sorry, and threw himself on the mercy of the court. Satisfied that the young fellow had learned his lesson, the Commander sentenced him to two weeks restriction to the base and three weeks KP in the base mess-hall.

As Personnel Officer, I was also in charge of the promotion of war bonds. I received a citation from Commander Head of the Eastern Sea Frontier because VPB-73 was participating 100 percent in War Bond purchases. We were the only squadron in the Eastern Sea Frontier to achieve that goal. What a reason for a citation!

ICED UP

Lieutenant Commander Dryden W. Hundley, our Executive Officer, believed in flying his share of patrols and anti-submarine sweeps. He steadfastly refused to allow desk work and administrative duties to keep him on the ground.

Though many of the VPB-73 pilots dreaded flying as his first or second pilot, I welcomed it. There was no one who knew as much about a Catalina as "Uncle John." If you were alert, you could learn a lot from him. I wanted to acquire as much knowledge as I could.

February over the North Atlantic is one of the most treacherous months of the year. Fog, snow, sleet and heavy icing conditions prevailed from the ocean's surface to many thousands of feet in the air.

On February 23rd, Lt. (jg.) Adelt and I were scheduled to fly a nighttime anti-submarine sweep with our Exec as PPC.

Departing Floyd Bennett at last light, we flew to Point X-Ray off Montauk Point and then took up a heading out to sea.

The outside air temperature was near freezing, and a layer of heavy, threatening clouds covered the sky. We were flying at our patrol altitude of 800 feet. Uncle John and I were in the cockpit, and Lt. (jg.) Adelt was in the nav comparment plotting the legs for our sweep. We were on instruments at the time, and radar was doing all of the searching.

Suddenly we penetrated a low-hanging curtain of clouds, and instantly the plane was iced up! A half inch of clear ice covered the windshield, and, though the deicer boots on the wings and tail were pulsating to break the ice formations loose, 73-P-4 became very sluggish. The propeller deicing fluid caused chunks of ice to separate from the props and slam noisily against the hull. The two Pratt-Whitneys roared in protest but continued to struggle to keep us in the air. I had no idea that it took such a short time, only seconds, to take on a load of ice!

Barely keeping airborne and hoping the pilot-heater kept working and that the venturis remained clear of ice, we slogged through the air. Radio reported that the ice-coated flat-top antennas had carried away, eliminating the CW high frequency radios. The MHF voice radio antenna still held. Seeking a warmer strata of air, we began a 180-degree turn, barely banking the wings, so as not to lose any lift. Arriving at the reciprocal heading, we made for the coastline.

Emerging from the ice storm, we were able to gain some altitude, and 73-P-4 became more manageable. The ice on the windshield still blocked any outside view, so Uncle John asked me for my sheath knife. Taking it, he pried open the triangular side ventilation windows and, reaching out into the sub-zero blast, gingerly chipped a hole in the ice. When he had a slit about three inches long and a half inch wide, he handed my knife back to me. Now he could see!

As we neared Floyd Bennett, still encrusted with the ice, we were able to climb to the traffic pattern altitude. Entering the pattern, we signaled the plane captain in the tower to lower the landing gear. Acknowledging the order, the light on the yoke flicked off, and we could see and feel the main gear lock into the down position. But, unfortunately, the nose wheel remained in the up position. The doors were frozen shut!

Uncle John called over the intercom, asking if there was any hot coffee left, and if so, to have someone climb into the nose compartment and pour it down the inspection panel to thaw the doors. Though it took all of the remaining coffee in the pot plus two more pots of boiling water to remove the ice from the nose-wheel doors, they were finally ice-free and they opened. We landed without further complications. Uncle John knew how to handle things!

As 73-P-4 was pulled into the hangar to defrost, I noticed that there were cones of ice about two feet long still on the propeller hubs, and that the blisters were still coated. We felt fortunate to have Uncle John as our PPC.

GARBAGE

The City of New York had two places that could be used to dispose of the tons of waste accumulated by its citizens. One location was the landfill of the proposed international airport on Long Island. When completed, it became known as Idlewild, and later, John F. Kennedy Airport.

The alternate disposal plan included the use of huge barges, towed or pushed out into the Atlantic by sea-going tugs. Once miles from shore, the garbage was dumped overboard, much to the delight of the myriad gulls that followed the procession seaward. Present-day ecologists would have had a field day over waste disposal in 1945.

This is the story of one of those barges.

One foggy morning in March, Bill Lee, Oren Marshall and I were standing by for a mission briefing.

As the ACI officer began telling us the details of our patrol, the phone rang. After a short conversation, ending with, "We'll find it," he hung up. A smile crossed his face.

He told us that the phone call was from the Port Authority of New York. Two tugs were towing six garbage scows out to sea. The fog we were experiencing at Floyd Bennett was much more dense at sea. A short time ago, he said, the fog had cleared a bit, and as they neared the Ambrose Light Ship, one of the men in charge of the scows decided to make an inspection tour. He gingerly felt his way over the piles of debris filling the barges, noting with pride the way things were going, when suddenly, his heart sank! Instead of six barges, there were only five in tow. One was missing! It had broken loose and was adrift without lights somewhere in the Atlantic. We were to locate it so it would cease to be a hazard to navigation.

Assigning our scheduled mission to the ready-duty crew, he gave us the last known position of the errant garbage scow and, with estimates of the current, its probable present location.

We took off and headed for the Ambrose Light Ship, the barge's last known position. The missing garbage carrier had been

1945

adrift for about ten hours. Following the oceanographic data furnished by the ACI officer, we soon were homing in on the drifting derelict. It was literally covered with gulls, thousands feasting on the heaps of waste, thousands more circling wanting to land, and that many more floating on the water picking up scraps the others had dropped! Since we could not remain over the scow until a tug arrived to take it in tow, we had our radioman notify Floyd Bennett that we had located it, were keeping it under surveillance, and recommended that a blimp from Lakehurst be sent to hover over the garbage-laden thing to enable the tug to home in on it. This the base agreed to do.

Three hours later a blimp arrived. Because we were not over a convoy, we talked to its Commander on the voice radio, telling him of the wandering barge. We could see the blimp pull up over the scow, throttle its two engines to idle, and remain almost stationary over the garbage with all of the gulls.

In order to get one last look at the flocks of birds swarming over and around the vessel, we flew by it at wave-top height. We were down-wind at the time, and we immediately discovered that we really didn't need radar to locate the thing; the stench it emitted would have betrayed its location in the densest of fogs or on the darkest of nights.

The smell didn't bother the gulls one bit; they enjoyed it.

JEEP CARRIER

In our sector of the world, we saw very few Navy pilots with battle decorations. With the exception of the awards given the crews for combat with the Fiats and the Focke-Wulf 200, only gold Navy Wings adorned the chests of the pilots of Patrol Squadron 73.

This was not so with the pilots and crews flying off the small escort carriers operating in the Atlantic, the *Bogue, Biter,* and *Archer.* Utilizing F4F Wildcats and TBF Avengers, the escort carriers caused the U-boats to lose control of the air gap in mid-Atlantic. These airmen, flying from carriers built on converted merchant vessel hulls, blasted the German subs with rockets, depth charges and machine guns. And they won.

Their awards were justly deserved.

Whenever the "baby flattops" dropped anchor in the Brooklyn Navy Yard for refitting or overhaul, the pilots invariably sought out the BOQ and Officers' Club at Floyd Bennett.

While all the world knows that fighter and torpedo pilots are the most glamorous fliers in the world (and they were quick to tell you about it), we P-boat pilots got our two bits in, too.

The anti-submarine war plans directed that Civil Air Patrol aircraft would conduct what was called "in-shore patrols," flying just offshore, no further than twenty-five miles to sea; from twenty-five to fifty miles offshore was the Coast Guard in its Grumman JRFs and Hall-Aluminum flying boats; blimps from the ZP squadron at Lakehurst patrolled from fifty to one hundred miles out; and the PBYs of VP-73 escorted the convoys from one hundred miles to five hundred miles. From the five hundred-mile point to five hundred miles from the European side, the escort carriers *Bogue, Biter* and *Archer* provided coverage. This continuous aerial escort defeated the U-boat in the Battle of the Atlantic.

Whenever we heard the VF or VT pilots declaiming their prowess, we P-boat pilots made it a point of honor to inform the braggart that we protected them for almost half of their voyage across the Atlantic. It didn't cause them to become abashed, but it did us good to let them know that we knew who was guarding whom.

On April 1, 1945, Marsh, Naj and I were scheduled for a coverage of the *Bogue* and sixteen merchantmen. We picked them up one hundred fifty miles out and were on them for eight hours until we were relieved by another of the squadron.

After a few hours of sweeping the sea around the convoy and the escort carrier, we became bored with the whole affair and decided to fly nearer the *Bogue* to get a better look at it, inasmuch as we had seen very little of aircraft carriers.

One of the rules of sea-air warfare is that no aircraft approach any ship, particularly a warship, head on—i.e., with the nose of the aircraft pointing directly at the vessel. This was to eliminate any possibility that the airplane was making an attack on the ship.

Naj was doing the flying, and as we circled the *Bogue,* he decided to get a better look, so he signaled the plane captain to lower the wing-tip floats, then turned toward the stern of the little carrier and headed toward it, a bit to one side, not straight on, at slow cruising speed.

As we neared the *Bogue,* we noticed a flurry of activity on the flight deck aft. Suddenly we saw what was going on, the LSO (Landing Signal Officer) had taken his position and was giving us signals with his paddles, as though we were going to land our PBY on the carrier deck. There was no way we could land our P-boat with its 104-foot wingspan on the 60-foot-wide flight deck of the *Bogue!* As if the LSO realized we never would fit on his deck, he put his hands on his hips, and watched us fly past. He looked very disgusted.

The Eastern Sea Frontier sent out dozens of memos advising all aircraft never to make landing approaches on any of the jeep carriers, with the direst consequences promised to any who did.

BRIDGES

Friday, April 13, 1945, broke bright and clear, but in every other respect it was Black Friday, for devastating news had come over the loudspeakers in the hangars and barracks.

"Attention! Attention! All hands! President Roosevelt is dead. Repeat, our Supreme Commander, President Roosevelt, is dead."

We were stunned. One of the plane Captains came up to Marsh and me and asked, "What will become of us now?" That query indicated that the Navy looked to Franklin Delano Roosevelt as their champion in peace, their leader in battle and their guarantee of a better world after victory.

Thirty days of mourning eliminated all comedians on the network radios, and funeral music filled every program.

According to the news stories both in the papers and on the radio, the burial would be at the Roosevelt family estate in Hyde

Park, New York, up the Hudson River from New York City. For several miles around, a restricted area had been established, banning all airplane flights by either the military or civilians.

On Sunday, April 15, Lt. (jg.) Marshall was scheduled for a training flight. He was my roommate. As he pulled on his flight gear, I noticed that he had a tourist-type chart in the knee pocket of his flying suit.

"Where you going?" I asked.

"Just around," he replied. Saying no more, he left for the flightline.

A few hours later, the phones at all of the offices at Floyd Bennett were ringing off the wall.

"A big Nazi airplane just flew under the George Washington Bridge!"

"Japanese zeroes are bombing the Statue of Liberty!"

"A squadron of enemy planes are attacking the Brooklyn Bridge!"

"I could see the meatballs on their wings real plain, y'know!"

Hundreds of phone calls tied up the circuits for hours as reports came in concerning the mysterious aircraft.

At around 1300, while going over to the squadron after chow, I saw a PBY enter the traffic pattern from the south and land. It was Marsh in 73-P-10, the ship we had flown to Africa. I'd know it anywhere.

I went back to the BOQ and awaited Marsh's return. As he came into the room, I asked, "Where you been?"

"Up flyin' around."

"You been up to Hyde Park?"

"Naw, we turned around at Poughkeepsie."

Just then we heard a radio blaring in the adjoining room. The announcer was telling of the puzzling flight. He stated that no accurate reports were available as to the type of plane, its number or markings. People saw swastikas, rising suns and not much else. But, said the announcer, the pilots of that plane thrilled thousands of onlookers as it flew down the Hudson River, under every one of the bridges, six or seven in all.

The reporter continued, "The pilots of that plane or planes can consider themselves lucky. For on each of those bridges spanning the Hudson are cable sway braces, running from the river banks to the center of each bridge. This is to keep the span from moving in the wind. Luckily the mysterious fliers went down the exact center of the river, missing the cables anchoring the bridge. Had the plane been only a few feet off the centerline, the heavy cables would have sheared off a wing."

Marsh turned a little white.

"Did you fly under all of those bridges?" I asked.

"Yep, and I'm not going to do it again."

That was all we ever said about the incident, and no one ever knew who was piloting the mystery plane except those in the crew. Until now.

U-235

By May of 1945, the war was going very badly for Nazi Germany. Hitler had committed suicide, Berlin had been taken and the entire Reich had collapsed. On May 7, 1945, Germany surrendered unconditionally to the Allied forces. The European war was over. The Allied Command, headed by General Dwight Eisenhower, in ordering the surrender of all German naval forces, decreed that all U-boats at sea were to surface immediately, to fly a black flag from their attack periscope denoting their surrender, and to remain in position until Allied vessels arrived. They were warned not to scuttle or sabotage their U-boats in any way.

On that day, the entire Eastern Sea Frontier was thrown into dismay. A U-boat surfaced ten miles off Cape May, New Jersey, flying a black flag, offering to surrender!

The whole staff of the ESF Office of Naval Intelligence was taken completely by surprise, for the U-boat had appeared in an area thought by ONI to be free of the underwater raiders! And it was but a few miles from New York Harbor!

All of us recalled the huge wall chart in the ACI briefing room with the convoy routes marked with colored flags and swastika flags denoting known U-boat locations. These locations ranged from the Bay of Biscay, off Iceland, to the mid-Atlantic, the Azores, Bermuda and dozens of other places; but none were plotted off Cape May. It is no wonder that the surfacing of the German raider caused such consternation!

A blimp and two destroyers were dispatched to the surrendering submarine, which identified itself as the U-235.

When the news of the surrendering U-boat reached the New York newspaper offices, the Floyd Bennett telephones rang constantly with requests that reporters and photographers be allowed on the scene.

Select teams of reporters and photographers were admitted to the base and were assigned to the various units. A group from a New York tabloid newspaper was assigned to VPB-73.

Greeted by the skipper, the newsmen were brought to the ready room, where Lts. (jg.) Oren Marshall, Art Smith and I were shooting a game of snooker. Seeing that we obviously needed to be engaged in a more productive pursuit, the skipper suggested we fly the guests out to see the U-235 and allow them to photograph it.

We gathered a flight crew, told them what we were going to do and advised them to take their cameras, as this was the only U-boat many of us had actually seen.

By the time we came upon the scene, several other ships had arrived, in addition to the blimp and circling aircraft. The gray undersea raider was awash, the crew standing on the deck and at positions in the conning tower and machine gun mounts on the bandstand aft on the tower.

We circled the U-235 several times to allow the tabloid photographers to take their pictures, and at the same time to allow the crew to snap theirs. Then, the photo session over, we returned to Floyd Bennett. As the reporters left, our crew took the exposed film from their Brownie cameras and hurried them to the base photo lab for developing.

A day or so later the fellows brought their pictures for Marsh, Smitty and me to see. The image of the U-boat was so small it was barely discernible. Even so, on the back of each was stamped in red ink, "OFFICIAL PHOTOGRAPH NOT TO BE USED FOR PUBLICATION. BY THE ORDER OF THE CHIEF OF THE BUREAU OF AERONAUTICS."

That Sunday, on the front page of that tabloid's edition, was a photograph of the U-235. It was full-page, and you could count the buttons on the crews' Kreigsmarine uniforms.

REDEPLOYED

With the end of the Hitler War, a massive relocation of American forces began. Japan remained a determined enemy.

On May 24, 1945, our squadron was ordered to San Juan, Puerto Rico, where its new assignment would be to fly air-sea rescue missions (Dumbo) along the flight paths of the returning Army Air Corps units. Within twenty-four hours the squadron was packed and ready for the move.

On the morning of our departure, as Uncle John Hundley, Lt. (jg.) George Adelt, and I were walking out to our plane, 73-P-2, we noticed our plane captain struggling with the Duty Officer's Cushman motor scooter. The crewman was back by the tunnel-gun hatch at the rear of the plane, trying to pick up the scooter and put it into the aft compartment.

In his determination and frustration at not being able to make the scooter pass through the confines of the tunnel hatch, he did not notice our approach.

"Need some help?" queried our Executive Officer. The straining crewman turned and, recognizing the interrogator, dropped the Cushman, and it clattered over on the cement ramp. The plane captain explained that he had "found" the scooter, and was afraid someone would steal it, so he thought that he'd better take it along to San Juan. Then, too, he explained, it would come in handy for quick transportation in Puerto Rico.

Uncle John took a dim view of his explanation. He informed the miscreant that he was on report, and then went on to point out that the Cushman in the extreme rear of 73-P-2 would have caused the plane to be dangerously tail heavy, and we could have stalled out on take-off and never known the reason the ship was out of trim. With that, the Exec dismissed the quaking crew chief.

The flight of the squadron from New York to San Juan included refueling stops at Morrison Field, Florida, and the naval base at Guantánamo Bay, Cuba.

Our quarters in San Juan were reminiscent of the movies I had seen of the homes of wealthy planters in the South Seas. Never had any of us lived in such swank. The only problem was that we weren't on the ground long enough to enjoy our new-found luxury. We were in the air constantly, practicing water landings, taking instrument refresher courses and patrolling along the Air Transport Command flight paths from Europe.

Despite the continuation of our intense flight activities along the ATC route, it was obvious that there was no future in remaining in a squadron in the Atlantic. I reluctantly applied for a transfer to some squadron in the Pacific area of operations. Though I was hesitant to leave all my shipmates in VPB-73, with whom I had flown since November of 1943, I asked for the transfer "for the good of the Navy." That last statement, I was told, ensured a reassignment.

My request was approved, and as the only passenger in a giant Martin JRM Mars flying boat, I was flown to Washington, D.C., and the Pentagon.

Never in my life had I seen so many high-ranking officers of all branches of the service. Generals and the like were a dime a dozen. Locating the Bureau of Aeronautics, I went up to the Personnel Department, where a WAVE greeted me politely and asked my business. I told her I wanted to see my orders for my new assignment. She asked my name and serial number, departed and returned in a few moments with my complete Navy file. That seemed quite a feat, considering the millions of Navy files stored there.

As I stood waiting for the WAVE's return, a Commander came up to me and said, "What are you looking for, young fellow?" I explained that I was seeking orders to the Pacific. He said, "When you get them and they don't satisfy you, come see me and I'll see that you're sent anyplace you want to go."

My orders were in my file. I was being transferred to Patrol Squadron 91, forming at Whidbey Island near Seattle. I was satisfied with the new duty, and anxiously awaited joining the new squadron.

Carlisle checked me out in
9/12/45 – PBY5A – # 48431
" " 48425
9/20/45 –
9/25/45 – PB2B-1 – 44223
10/5/45 – PBY5A – 34026

VP-91

Following receipt of my orders directing me to VP-91, I was given a thirty-day leave. For the first time ever, I flew United Airlines from Washington, D.C. to Omaha. The entire flight was at night, and I was impressed by the night landings those United pilots made. They landed those DC-3s so gently it was impossible to tell when the wheels touched down. The landings we made after dark could definitely be heard and felt!

I reported to the squadron on July 27 and was assigned a crew immediately. Since I was already a PPC, there was no need for further check rides. It was almost like returning to an old friend, for during the two ferrying flights when we delivered the Russian PBNs we had landed there prior to departing for Kodiak.

A pleasant surprise awaited me when I got down to the flight line. There I discovered that we were being assigned new PBY-6As.

The 6A was the latest model in the PBY series. Though it still basically represented the previous types, it contained a few differences. It had a higher rudder, and the hull configuration was that of the Naval Aircraft Factory's PBN-1. The new design also had additional armor, armament and radar. Above all, we appreciated the push-button radios! No more would we have to twist the crank to tune the "coffee grinders" in an endeavor to find the proper radio frequency. Now we merely had to punch the proper button and the station was automatically dialed in. How modern could you get?

VP-91 was being refitted, having returned from the South Pacific a few months ago. It had been in a lot of action, both in Black Cat operations and in Dumbo flights.

We had hardly begun reforming when the world received the news that the *Enola Gay* had dropped the first atomic bomb on Japan on August 6, 1945.

Before the significance of that event was fully realized, the 20th Air Force's B-29 Bock's Car had dropped another of the bombs on the Japanese city of Nagasaki. On August 15, Japan surrendered, and the war was over.

Flight operations continued unabated, although it seemed more and more of the airplanes were out of commission due to maintenance problems. It was almost impossible to find a P-boat that didn't have a yellow sheet full of discrepancies. Within a short time it was doubtful if any of the Catalinas would be airworthy. But with peace, nobody cared anymore, it seemed.

In spite of the shortcomings we experienced with the airworthiness of our planes, we still had to fly. Scuttlebutt had it that we were to be part of the occupation forces in Japan or Korea.

One night the entire squadron was engaged in water-landing practice. Everything was going smoothly until about 2100, when the crash boat monitoring the flights reported driftwood and debris floating into the landing area. We had to cease further water operations and divert to NAS Seattle. At that time there was no land-based facility on Whidbey Island.

We all proceeded to Seattle and landed without incident. The planes were secured and we were assigned quarters in the transient barracks.

During the night it rained heavily.

Early the next morning all of us prepared to depart for the flight to Whidbey Island. Dozens of other planes, PBYs, PVs and R4Ds were lined up on the runway. Responding to orders from the tower, I pulled ahead and turned slightly, in order to go around a PV in front of us. In doing so, the starboard main landing gear wheel went off the paved surface and onto the shoulder, and in a second the wheel sank hub-deep in the soft soil. I was stuck in the mud!

Shutting down the engines, I called the tower, told them the problem and we all got out of the plane. It took two giant wreckers with booms and twelve men plus my crew to get the plane out of the mud. That was my last flight as a P-boat pilot.

POTPOURRI

Once the airplane was extracted from the mud, it was hosed down and the starboard brake line was found to be damaged. My crew and I hitched rides in other planes of the squadron and flew back to Whidbey Island.

The day after my return, October 27, 1945, I awoke with a very severe stomach ache. Upon reporting to the dispensary, it was discovered that I had acute appendicitis. I was taken by ambulance to the naval hospital at Seattle, where my appendix was removed.

Following a period of convalescence, I was released from the hospital, and, because I had enough points for immediate discharge, I received orders to report to the Naval Air Station at Grosse Ile, Illinois, for separation.

On December 7, 1945, I arrived back home, in Norfolk, Nebraska, exactly four years after my brother Orv had called to tell me about Pearl Harbor.

My brother Orv had been reclassified 4F by the Selective Service Board. In my mind he had the toughest job of anyone in not being allowed to serve in the military services. He did exemplary work in seeing that servicemen home on leave had a proper welcome. Upon my return, Orv and I went into the shoe business, working together until 1988, when he passed away. He was a good brother.

My brother Frank, Jr., served as a B-25 pilot in the 17th Reconnaissance Squadron of the 5th Air Force in the South Pacific. On January 9, 1945, the day American forces invaded the Philippines, Frank had been shot down while attacking Clark Field near Manila. He was missing in action until April. The folks were notified on April 13, 1945 (the day FDR died) that he and his crew and their plane had been found by the guerillas in northern Luzon. Frank is buried in the military cemetery in the Philippines.

I had planned on making the Navy my career. All of my papers were in and recommendations for USN were approved by our squadron officers. But when Frank was lost I decided I had better withdraw my USN application and get home to help the folks out. This I did.

The reader will notice that no accounting has been made here of the activities with members of the distaff side. But be assured that the P-boat pilots of VP-73 were much aware of the opposite sex's existence. The suite at the Belmont Plaza Hotel in Manhattan will attest to that.

My log book shows that I made over one hundred operational flights against the U-Bootwaffe (AS patrols, convoy escort, maritime reconnaissance), the flights averaging fourteen hours in length. No flight was ever aborted by my crew due to aircraft discrepancies or foul weather.

In addition to the operational missions mentioned above, all of the crews flew training and familiarization hops and ferry missions when assignments were made.

The flight crews were given one day off a week. The pilots in my crew had an agreement that we would tour the night spots the night of our day of liberty; during the day we would visit museums, art galleries and the like. That way we were in shape to fly upon our return from liberty.

With the flight in the PBY-6A to Seattle, my days of being a P-boat pilot came to an end. I hated to see them over.

VE-VJ DAY

Do those of you that have not flown
Know the joy to be alive?
To have the sky your very own,
To soar and curve and dive.
If you've never sailed the airy space,
You've missed the surge of power,
The coarse wind blasting by your face.
'Midst the fleecy clouded bower.
We've flown above the churning sea,
Through fog and sleet and haze.
Beneath our broad wings, ships below,
Escaped the U-boat's gaze.
No more we'll hear the song of speed,
As our propellers race,
For us, they say, there's no more need,
World peace is now in place.

Lt. Robert L. Carlisle, USNR
15 August 1945

Glossary

Aft	Rear; in back of
Aldis lamp	Signal lamp used to transit Morse code.
Aviation Cadet Selection Board	Selectors of candidates for Aviation Cadet training; for the central United States, its location was Kansas City, Missouri.
Bandstand	Extra platforms built on the conning towers of U-boats on which were mounted additional machine guns and flak cannon to be used against aircraft.
Black Cat	A PBY used in night operations, usually painted a dull black for night camouflage. Used primarily in the South Pacific.
CPT	Civilian Pilot Training. A flight course sponsored by the government to train pilots for the growing air forces of the United States.
Coffee grinder	WWII airborne radio tuned by turning a handle very similar to the crank on a kitchen appliance used to grind coffee beans.
Dead reckoning (D.R.)	Navigating by using wind drift, wind estimation, and time to determine position.

Ditch	Abandon the aircraft, as in a forced landing.
Dumbo	Air-sea rescue operations. Named after the elephant in the Walt Disney movie.
Duty Officer	Squadron officer assigned this temporary post, in charge for term of responsibility, usually twenty-four hours.
FAA	Federal Aviation Administration. Replaced the CAA (Civil Aeronautics Administration) after WWII.
Fiat	Italian-built biplane fighter used extensively in the Spanish Civil War. Many were exported by Italy. Similar in configuration to the Stearman N2S.
Focke-Wulf 200C	Four-engine German long-range bomber used with U-boats and in an anti-shipping role. Later used as transports in Russia by the Luftwaffe.
Ground school	Academic study of aviation courses.
Head	Toilet.
Kingfisher (OS2U)	Vought Aircraft used as a scout plane, catapulted from the stern of cruisers and battleships.
Liberty	Time off, usually twenty-four to forty-eight hours.
Mast	A type of court martial held before the Commanding Officer of a unit.
Morane Saulnier	A French fighter manufactured in about 1938.
NAS	Naval Air Station.
NATC	Naval Air Training Center, or Command. Usually Pensacola, Florida, or Corpus Christi, Texas.

GLOSSARY

Nav	Compartment aft of cockpit holding the Navigation Officer and his equipment.
OS2U	*See* Kingfisher.
P-boat	Patrol Seaplane, especially a Consolidated PBY Catalina.
PBY	Twin-engined flying boat built by consolidated, P patrol; B bomber; Y Consolidated (Navy designation).
PV-1	Fast twin-engine medium bomber manufactured by Lockheed.
Secondary	Advanced CPT teaching aerobatics.
SNV-1	*See* Vultee.
Spin	An aerial maneuver caused by the loss of flying speed.
Solo	A student pilot's first time in the air alone; a pilot's milestone.
Sub-squad	Cadets who were unable to pass first tests and are being given extra instruction to enable them to pass.
TBD	Obsolete torpedo bombers built by Douglas. Used by Torpedo Squadron 8.
TBF	Torpedo bomber built by Grumman.
UPF-7	Waco-built biplane used in advanced civilian pilot training.
Vega	Fast Lockheed plane, similar to the ship flown by Wiley Post.
Vega Ventura	*See* PV-1.
VIP	Very Important Person; High Brass; Ranking officer
VP	Navy Designation of heavier-than-air squadron whose job is patrol.

Vultee	SNV-1 training plane used in advanced training. Another type built by Vultee, called the Vindicator, was used by the Free French in photo operations.
Waco	*See* UPF-7.
WAVEs	Female members of the Navy; a woman sailor.
X-Ray	An arbitrary point plotted on a chart denoting a point of departure.
Yellow Peril	Stearman N2S training plane, usually painted a bright yellow for visibility.
Yoke	Structure to which the pilot's and co-pilot's control wheel was attached.
Zinderneuf	Fort in the novel *Beau Geste*.